THE
FIXER

THE
FIXER

My Adventures

Saving Startups from Death by Politics

BRADLEY TUSK

PENGUIN / PORTFOLIO

Portfolio/Penguin
An imprint of Penguin Random House LLC
375 Hudson Street
New York, New York 10014

Most Portfolio books are available at a discount when purchased in quantity for sales promotions or corporate use. Special editions, which include personalized covers, excerpts, and corporate imprints, can be created when purchased in large quantities. For more information, please call (212) 572-2232 or email specialmarkets@penguinrandomhouse.com. Your local bookstore can also assist with discounted bulk purchases using the Penguin Random House corporate Business-to-Business program. For assistance in locating a participating retailer, email B2B@penguinrandomhouse.com.

Illustrations by Shyama Golden

Library of Congress Cataloging-in-Publication Data

Names: Tusk, Bradley, author.
Title: The fixer : my adventures saving startups from death by politics / Bradley Tusk.
Description: New York City : Portfolio, 2018.
Identifiers: LCCN 2018015642| ISBN 9780525536499 (hardback) |
ISBN 9780525536505 (ebook)
Subjects: LCSH: New business enterprises. | New business enterprises—
Government policy. | New business enterprises—Law and legislation. |
BISAC: BUSINESS & ECONOMICS / Government & Business. |
POLITICAL SCIENCE / Public Policy / Economic Policy. |
BUSINESS & ECONOMICS / New Business Enterprises.
Classification: LCC HD62.5 .T877 2018 | DDC 658.1/1—dc23
LC record available at https://lccn.loc.gov/2018015642

Printed in the United States of America
3 5 7 9 10 8 6 4 2

Book design by Laura K. Corless

For Harper, Abigail, and Lyle

Contents

SECTION V

Where Do We Go from Here?

SECTION I

When Travis Fought Bill

1

Turns Out You Can Fight City Hall

allas–Fort Worth airport is a fairly miserable place to be on a good day. When it's raining cats and dogs and flights to LaGuardia are being wiped off the board, DFW is a solid contender for the ninth circle of hell. I was sitting at a United gate, hoping for a standby seat on the one flight to New York not yet canceled. My phone lit up. Travis.

Travis Kalanick, at the time, was the cofounder and CEO of Uber. We had been working together since 2011, fighting off attempts by the taxi industry to prevent ridesharing from existing—Travis in his role as CEO and me as the founder and CEO of Tusk Strategies, a political consulting firm based in New York. We'd managed, so far, to keep taxis at bay and break into every market in the United States. But all of a sudden, in the summer of 2015, we found ourselves facing a new front in the war.

"You see what de Blasio just did?"

"No. I'm stuck at DFW. What'd he do this time?"

"Announced he wants to cap our growth at one percent a year. Basically kills the business. Go check it out online and call me back."

I did some quick research. *Politico,* the *Daily News,* and the *Times* all had stories. Travis was right. (I'd been hoping he was exaggerating.) Bill de Blasio, New York City's mayor, had just proposed legislation that would kill Uber's growth and operations. De Blasio had been in office for around eighteen months and, at that point, exerted full and complete control over the fifty-one-member city council who'd be voting on Uber's future. He hated technology, hated business, hated the private sector, and was as responsive to the whims and needs of his campaign donors (in this case, the taxi medallion owners) as the city council was to his. Not a good dynamic.

Two minutes later, Travis and I talked again.

"This is bad," I told him.

"No shit. If it happens in New York, the whole world is going to see it. Which means it could happen anywhere. We can't let that happen."

"Travis, a close city council vote is 49–2; 48–3 is considered a nail-biter. We need twenty-six votes to beat this. There's a reason they say you can't fight city hall."

"Then figure out how to get us twenty-six votes."

"Okay." I paused, thinking. "Two questions: How much can I spend and is there any argument I can't use?"

"Whatever you need."

My mind started spinning with possibilities. The flight, miraculously, started boarding and, even more miraculously, I got off the standby list and onto the plane. Middle seat in the row right next to the bathroom, but at least I was heading home—with a pretty big problem to figure out before I got there.

It may seem hard to imagine today, when "to Uber somewhere" has become a verb, but Uber wasn't always inevitable. As a fledgling startup attempting to disrupt the taxi industry, it faced challenges from regulators left and right. Labor hated it because it was impossible to control, much less organize, thousands of freelance contractors. The taxi industry hated it because it took only one on-demand, seamlessly transacted Uber ride for customers to switch their loyalty forever. Politicians across the country hated it because Uber's success just meant being screamed at by their donors in the taxi industry.

The stakes were high. If Uber was unable to operate freely in America's most important financial and cultural center, it was almost a precedent for legislators all over the world to shut us down. We were fucked without New York—there was no way to justify Uber's high valuation, its investors' lofty expectations, and its promises of changing the way people get around if we couldn't freely operate in the world's most visible city.

As I sat there on the tarmac waiting for takeoff, I thought hard about the man standing between us and Uber's future. Bill de Blasio became mayor of New York City in 2013 by portraying himself as a champion of the left, as the antagonist of income inequality, as the hero of people of color. He structured every fight, every policy, every issue as "de Blasio, champion of the oppressed versus big, bad corporation." The politics worked well for him, since it forced virtually every union, newspaper, pundit, political influencer, and everyone else in the system to take his side or risk being thrown out of the progressive mafia. His play was clearly going to be "de Blasio defending poor taxi drivers against the big, bad, multibillion-dollar Uber." And that play had a very good chance of success.

We had to come up with a different story.

I thought hard about de Blasio's pain points. He wasn't acting from an honest place of belief or ideology—just cold, hard, pay-to-play politics. But that was true of virtually every mayor in every city. Voters were used to it.

Somewhere over the Ozarks, the answer hit me. De Blasio had a weakness—one he was dangerously unaware of. No one had tried pressing that weakness before, but if it worked, it could upend all of the conventional wisdom, including that centuries-old adage about not being able to fight city hall. Sure, it would be an uphill political battle—risky and possibly costing Uber an embarrassing loss on a global stage. But it was our only shot.

Confession: Uphill political fights are kind of my thing. I learned how to handle them by working in government and politics for more than two decades for the good, the bad, and the ugly. I ran Mike Bloomberg's New York mayoral campaign in 2009 and worked for him at city hall during his first term. I spent two years on Capitol Hill as Chuck Schumer's communications director, learning how to move the media at the feet of the most press-hungry and media-savvy politician in America. I spent four insane years as deputy governor of Illinois. The upside was that I got to run the fifth-biggest state in the nation—run its $60 billion budget, all state operations, oversee all seventy thousand state employees, all policy decisions, all legislation, and all communications—at the ripe age of twenty-nine. The downside was my boss was Rod Blagojevich. And along the way, I worked for local political legends like Henry Stern, New York City's longtime zany and brilliant parks commissioner, and Ed Rendell, during his tenure as mayor of Philadelphia, and had a front-row seat to the heroic efforts of people like Rudy Giuliani, Chuck Schumer, Hillary Clinton, and Mike Bloomberg to rebuild New York City in the aftermath of 9/11.

I've had the chance to pioneer some truly meaningful and innovative policies—like universal preschool, universal health care for kids, a cashless tollway system, importing prescription drugs from Europe and Canada, modernizing the nation's voting systems, and offering radical transparency at city hall—and I also found myself viciously knocking Anthony Weiner out of a mayoral race, being asked to extort Rahm Emanuel, and testifying in three corruption trials and two grand juries.

I fell into tech by accident. After starting a consulting firm, I was sitting in a meeting one afternoon about Walmart's zoning issues. The phone rang and a friend of mine said, "Hey. There's a guy with a small transportation startup. He's having some regulatory problems. Would you mind talking to him?" I became Uber's first political adviser that same day and spent much of the next five years kicking the shit out of the taxi industry all over the United States to make ridesharing legal everywhere. I also made a bet that paid off pretty well, taking half my fee from Uber in equity when the startup was still in its infancy, a bet that ultimately produced a 250-fold return.

After the fight with de Blasio in 2015, I made another bet and turned my experience with Uber into a venture capital business. Now, at Tusk Ventures, we work with dozens of startups in regulated industries to protect them from politics. We also raised a fund and now invest in some of those startups too.

Startups disrupt industries through their ideas. Industries fight back through their connections. Just like a good startup's job is to blow up an industry, our job is to blow up the attempts to keep startups out of the market in the first place—to use the same techniques you see in campaigns and apply them to political and regulatory battles between startups and entrenched interests.

If you're in the system, you usually just live by the rules of engagement, and after a while, our dysfunctional brand of politics all seems perfectly normal to you. And if you're a typical business and you're regulated by the system (almost every industry is regulated, either directly or indirectly, by government at some level), you've learned the rules of engagement and you live with them.

But if you're a startup and politics is a completely foreign concept to you, none of this makes much sense. You just want to bring your product to market. You want to compete, you want to innovate, you want to disrupt. You don't want to be told by some bureaucrat what you can and can't do. And you really don't want to be told you can't compete just because the politics don't work in your favor.

If you're trying to disrupt almost any traditional industry—transportation, energy, health care, education, insurance, finance, hospitality, alcohol, beauty, gaming, housekeeping—they typically don't thank you for the disruption. They punch back, and they punch hard.

If you want a different outcome for your startup than death by regulators, you have to make it happen. The political and regulatory ecosystem has evolved over time to perpetuate itself, and the money that fuels it comes in the form of donations from the people you're disrupting. And those people—whether it's the taxi industry, hotel owners, casino owners, labor unions, insurance companies, you name it—are going to use whatever leverage they have to keep you at bay. Your competitive advantage is intellectual—your ideas, your technology, your approach to doing something differently, something better. Their competitive advantage is political—the campaign donations they've been doling out for years and the army of lobbyists on their payroll whose only job is to stop you.

The point of this book is to help startups think intelligently about politics so they can counterpunch or, ideally, avoid getting hit in the first place. The more you understand why politicians and regulators don't want you to launch a new hotel system, a new transportation network, or a new peer-to-peer insurance pool without their consent, the easier it is to figure out how to change the political equation and convince them to go along.

Just so we're clear, startup culture has a lot of growing up to do. The lack of diversity is not only unfair, it hurts the startups and venture capital funds trying to figure out how to sell their product or service to as many consumers as possible (white men are not the entirety of the market). The lack of maturity has created harmful workplaces. A lot needs to change. But none of that means that startups should stop standing up for themselves when it comes to politics. Entrenched interests are going to do everything they can to stifle competition and innovation. Failure to fight back is fatal.

I've organized this book into five sections. Section I and II tell the story of my political education, starting with Ed Rendell and ending with the Bloomberg mayoral campaign of 2009. Section III covers my first foray into tech with Uber, fighting city halls across the United States. Section IV shares the stories and lessons of helping startups avoid death by politics, like legalizing online daily fantasy sports (FanDuel and DraftKings), disrupting Big Insurance (Lemonade), and making it safe to get on-demand marijuana (Eaze).

Not every battle can be won, as I learned the hard way with a kitchen-sharing platform called MyTable. And some battles become so prolonged and complex that they involve throwing ourselves into the mess known as Trump and Washington, D.C. (Like I learned with Handy.) The last section offers a solution for all of this—mobile voting. Exponentially increasing participation by making it much easier to vote seems fairly obvious to you and me, but it also scares the shit out of just about every politician in power from both parties who have no interest in making it easier to unseat them. It'll make fighting city hall look like a Sunday-afternoon nap.

At the end of the book, there's a point-by-point guide for startups navigating particular scenarios, like trying to decide whether to ask for permission or beg for forgiveness, or how to mobilize your customers to help you fight political battles, or how to decide which market to break into next.

Sure, war stories about helping Tesla, taking out Anthony Weiner, reelecting Mike Bloomberg, navigating corrupt politics in Chicago, figuring out how to make weed delivery legal, taking on casinos and creating an uprising among fantasy sports nuts, and helping Uber get off the ground, among many others, are fun. (Hopefully you'll enjoy reading them as much as I enjoyed writing them.) But it's a lot more than that. Disrupting your industry doesn't just come with a better idea or a better platform. It means disrupting the political status quo too. Your employees, investors, and customers are counting on it. Your startup's future may depend on it. Long term, so does our economy. And in many ways, whether it's the chance technology offers to create new jobs, to make people's lives easier and better, or to develop a new approach to elections that can actually represent the people as a whole, our collective future does too.

SECTION II

Learning the Language
of Politics

2

No One Gives You Anything by Accident

Learning the language of politics (or the dark arts, as my wife, Harper, likes to call it) took a few years. I stumbled into politics almost by accident and half the opportunities that came along the way seemed equally random. But like any skill, with enough work, enough time, and enough repetition, you start to get pretty good at it.

I met Ed Rendell at the Democratic Convention in 1992. He was the mayor of Philadelphia (and later went on to serve as governor of Pennsylvania). I was a kid—I'd just finished my freshman year of college at Penn and was spending the summer working as a cabana boy at the Sands Beach Club on Long Island. If you remember the movie *The Flamingo Kid,* my job was a lot like that, except without the MILFs and semiprofessional poker games.

I spent six days a week getting people turkey burgers, iced coffees, and LEOs (lox, eggs, and onions, the highest-priced item on any beach club menu), filling inflatable pools, schlepping beach chairs down to the ocean, and making chitchat with the cabana renters, all of whom seemed like big shots to me.

I didn't know anyone in politics. My father came to the United States straight from the refugee camps in Germany after World War II, and while my family made a pretty good go of it in the *schmata* business (the garment business, for those of you who don't speak Yiddish), we weren't connected in any way. Except my dad knew one guy—Brian O'Dwyer—whose law firm represented the carpenters' union. Brian had a history in New York City politics (his dad had been city council president and his uncle was mayor for a brief time in the late '40s before facing a corruption scandal and relocating to Mexico) and he knew I wanted to get in the game.

In 1992 , the game was Bill Clinton. The Democratic Convention was taking place at Madison Square Garden, so the carpenters were charged with building the stage and getting the venue ready. That somehow gave the union a set of passes to use as they saw fit. One of those passes made their way from the union to Brian to me. "Just pretend to fix something if someone asks," he told me.

I've now been to enough political conventions to know that nothing really happens until the heavy hitters take the stage and the national TV cameras start rolling at around 8 p.m. But if you look in the newspaper, it says "Convention: noon to midnight." So as far as I knew, noon it was. I put on a suit, picked up the carpenters' pass from Brian's office downtown, and headed over to the Garden.

For an arena that seats nearly twenty thousand, there couldn't have been more than five hundred people in the entire place. Two guys running for state rep in Montana (or something at that level) were speaking to a crowd of no one. The seats were empty. Except there was one guy sitting there. And he looked familiar.

At first, I wasn't sure if it was okay to go talk to him. He was the mayor after all. But then I thought, *He's the mayor of Philly, I go to school in Philly. He's a Jewish guy from New York. So am I. I'll go say hi. What's the worst that can happen?* Turns out, Ed Rendell was so friendly, so gregarious, that if someone didn't come up to him to say hi, he would have just started talking to the empty seat next to him.

We talked about the usual stuff—what I was studying at school, how I liked Penn, what he thought of Clinton's chances in the general—and after around ten minutes, I figured I'd taken enough of his time so I thanked him and he said, "Are you busy when you get back to school?"

I thought about it for a moment and answered honestly: "No, not really."

"Well, do you want be an intern in our office?"

Of course I did. He told me to send him a letter and he'd have someone set it up.

I was so excited, I barely noticed the rest of the day. I wrote the letter on a fistful of Zaro's Bread Basket napkins on the Long Island Rail Road trip home, typed it up the next morning, and sent it to city hall. I knew it'd take a few days to get a response, so I didn't start regularly checking the mailbox for a reply until later that week. It was at least a full five days before I started checking it obsessively. Nothing. What I know now, but didn't know then, is that correspondence is the black hole of government: Everything comes in, nothing comes out. But at the time, I thought either my letter or the reply must have gotten lost in the mail.

Summer ended. Most of the cabana owners were generous with their end-of-summer tips, except for one family who not only didn't tip, they stiffed me and skipped out on their food bill. (The Sands would make the cabana boys lay out the money for everyone's food and then collect from the customers.) There should be a special circle of hell for people who screw over cabana boys working seventy hours a week in the sun for tips and laying out cash they don't have just so the Tannenbaums don't have to pay for their egg white scramble in real time.* Despite them, I made enough money to last the school year, which meant an unpaid internship was financially possible.

I got back to school, moved into the dorms, bought some books, and then decided, "I still really want to work at city hall. Maybe I'll just go see him." In fairness to me, walking up to him the last time had worked. So I hopped on the SEPTA and took the train to city hall. This was almost a decade before 9/11, so security then wasn't what it is now. I walked into city hall and started wandering around until I saw a sign for the mayor's office. No one stopped me.

Now that I've walked past the outer office of a mayor or governor or senator thousands of times to get to and from my office, I know that only two types of people show up and ask to see the officeholder: crazy people or people protesting something. I got to Rendell's outer office. The desk was manned by two blue-haired older women from South Philly. I walked up and asked if the mayor was available. It took them a moment to reply because they were trying to figure out which of the two categories I belonged to. I seemed young and naïve, but not actually crazy. And I wasn't carrying a box of protest letters or a petition. I was exactly what I looked like: a nice young kid who was so clueless, he didn't realize you can't just show up at city hall and ask to see the mayor.

If they'd just blown me off and sent me on my way, my life may have turned out very differently. Fortunately, one of the old ladies smiled and said, "He's not available right now. Would you like to leave a note?"

So in my best chicken scratch, I wrote down who I was, why I was there, and that he probably didn't remember but we'd met at the Democratic Convention and he told me to write to him about an internship. They very nicely took the note and I headed back to the subway.

---

* Since the statute of limitations for peeing in someone's cooler has probably expired, I'll admit I did eventually get my revenge on the Tannenbaums, especially when they were wondering why the ice in their Diet Coke tasted funny. Over the years, this proved to be a lot like politics.

It wasn't till about halfway home that I realized, "You fucking idiot. You can't just show up and ask for the mayor. This is never going to happen." And by the time I got back to the dorm, I had pretty much abandoned my city hall dreams. Then the phone rang. "Hold for Mayor Rendell." I waited maybe twenty seconds, then this gravelly, booming voice came through the other line.

"Bradley?"

"Yes, sir."

"When are you coming to work?"

"I'll be there in twenty minutes."

And that was how it began. Obviously, he wasn't planning to meet with me twenty minutes later—or anytime really—but this time, he did have someone follow up with me and I was given an internship in the Office of the Deputy Mayor for Policy and Planning. And maybe it was because I was grateful that Rendell took the time to follow up or maybe because I realized that people as generous as Brian O'Dwyer don't come around that often or maybe just because it was a lot better than setting up beach umbrellas, whatever the reason, I knew I was being given a rare opportunity—and I was all in.

3

Control the Narrative, Control Politics

f Rendell's team had asked me to spend my time making copies and coffee, I wouldn't have minded. It was still a way in. But luckily, they decided to throw a few projects at the bottom of their to-do list my way.

One of those projects was to find a way to bring more talent into Philadelphia city government. New York City already had a program like that, so I met with a few New York City officials during my research. About halfway through the meeting, they looked at me and asked, "How old are you?"

When I explained I was in my junior year of college, one of them said, "You should apply to us. We even have a summer program for students heading into their senior year of college." I was about to head to Madrid to spend a semester abroad, so I dashed off an application and promptly forgot about it. A few months later, I got a letter telling me I'd been accepted and a few weeks after that, I met StarQuest.

Henry Stern is now fading from political lore, but for a twenty-five-year period, he was a New York City legend. Brought up in an immigrant household in Inwood at the upper tip of Manhattan, he shot his way through City College (then considered the Harvard for poor, white Jews from New York City), then Harvard Law School (some say he's the youngest graduate ever), and then threw himself into New York City politics, working for former Miss America Bess Myerson, who had become a prominent local politician. Henry eventually got elected to the city council, deploying a fund-raising strategy that revolved around looking through the phone book for names that sounded Jewish or familiar, calling them, and asking for help or money. Somehow, it worked.

In 1983, Mayor Ed Koch named Henry as parks commissioner, a job he'd been born to do.* To Henry, the trees were his constituents, the animals his friends, the parks themselves his personal property. Whenever we'd walk around a city park, he'd pick up trash as if it were his own living room. And when picking up trash isn't above the boss, it isn't above anyone.†

The Government Scholars program allowed you to work at any city agency for the summer. Most of the kids in the program had very high-minded goals for their stint in city government. They were going to

---

* He was removed from the job by Mayor Dinkins but then reinstated four years later by Mayor Giuliani.

† Henry also instilled an incredible sense of civic pride among almost everyone who worked at the Parks Department. All 8.5 million New York City residents use city parks in one way or another. If we did our jobs well, that meant the parks were cleaner and safer, and that directly improved everyone's quality of life. If the parks were dirty and dangerous, quality of life declined. Our job really mattered. Henry used it to motivate us to work twice as hard as we (legally) had to.

fight homelessness and poverty. My time in Philly had taught me better: It didn't matter what the agency did, what mattered were the people working there. Lazy or ineffective or unimaginative bureaucrats weren't worth working for, no matter how noble their agency's mission. I went from agency to agency, and the minute Henry said to me, "If you come here, I'll give you real work to do," I knew I'd found the right place.

I didn't know myself well enough at the time to realize this, but intuitively, I wanted two things from my work: a lot of action and to feel important. Henry's eleven-word promise covered both.

Like most politicians, Henry was obsessed with getting publicity. It was his oxygen. It validated his existence, proved his worth, prolonged his relevance. He also understood that if Parks—which, in terms of its budget, was a relatively tiny city agency—was constantly in the news, he could outpunch his weight and command more resources from other politicians who were equally desperate for attention. Why? Because if he can get a city councilman a soundbite on TV by coming up with a clever way to promote the local playground he funded, that councilman is a lot more likely to keep investing his discretionary budget into the thing that gets him attention.

That was when one of the cardinal rules of politics became clear: The vast majority of people who run for office are desperately insecure, often even self-loathing. They need attention and validation at all costs. Running for and holding office is the only way most of them can get it (since they typically lack the talent to meaningfully succeed at anything in the real world). Filling that hole in their psyche matters far more than anything else, so their first—and frequently only—rule is to preserve and enhance their chance of re-election.

The more press we got, the more Henry trusted my instincts. And the more he trusted me, the crazier and crazier shit we pulled.* The more we did that, the more reporters also trusted my instincts. (They have to cover a lot of ground in a limited amount of time, so if they knew that the press guy at Parks always had good stuff, his events got priority.) And that all created a virtuous cycle whereby taking care of Henry, the local press corps, and the local politicians, I could ensure we got the attention we needed to help turn our policy ideas into reality.

Of course, some of our stunts were simply designed to generate attention for the sake of attention (i.e., to make Henry happy), like the time we dressed Henry up as a groundhog, buried him in a park in Queens, and when the press came to cover our Groundhog's Day event, Henry popped out of the ground. (The front page of *Newsday* the next day was the picture of Henry's head popping up with the headline "Flakes in the Forecast.")

Some were designed to drive attention to corporate partners paying for Parks initiatives that we couldn't afford to fund from taxpayer revenue. We convinced EarthLink to pay us $125,000 to become "the official Internet Service Provider of the Parks Department." We used that money to pay to build a new website to help New Yorkers take advantage of everything offered at their parks. We owed EarthLink attention and media coverage in return.

So we built a forty-foot-by-forty-foot giant spiderweb of rope in

---

* That trust extended to representing the Parks Department at official events. One time in the mid-'90s, a newly elected foreign leader from Latin America was coming to New York and wanted to have a photo op at the Simón Bolívar statue on Central Park South. For whatever reason, neither the mayor nor Henry were available, so somehow, the job fell to me and our press secretary, Bob Lawson. When the dynamic young leader, who seemed fine with our being the highest-ranking representatives from the City of New York, asked what we did, in my best Spanish I stammered and then said "Parks worker." He liked that. As the event ended, he looked at Bob and me, raised his right arm in salute, and said *"Muchachos!"* We raised our arms back. Hugo Chávez turned out to be a murderous dictator, but he was pretty nice that afternoon.

Times Square. We dressed Henry in a sequined silver suit and top hat, put him on a riser obscured by dry ice, and blasted the theme song to *2001: A Space Odyssey* out of the giant speaker they use for New Year's Eve as he ascended the web to launch the new Parks Department website, paid for by EarthLink.

The same approach worked for policy initiatives. We staged elaborate funerals for trees murdered by people (cut down illegally by construction crews or poisoned by people who thought their views were obstructed by trees). One time, Henry chained himself to a tree in Union Square Park to try to prevent its demise. This all helped fuel legislation through the city council making arborcide a crime.

Of course, many of the shenanigans that made Parks such a fun place to work didn't impact the public one way or another. Henry's self-appointed moniker was StarQuest (*Stern* means "star" in German and Quest because he asked a lot of questions), and he gave out another twelve thousand Parks names to employees, friends, politicians, civic leaders, gadflies, and anyone else in the Parks ecosystem willing to take one.* He also tried to propel his golden retriever, Boomer, into the *Guinness Book of World Records* by making him the most-petted dog ever. They got to ten thousand pets, but the champion—a mutt from Maryland named Josh—was still out of reach. Henry's inherent wackiness sometimes made Parks a maddening place to work, but more than anything, it showed that government and politics can be a welcoming bastion for talented, creative people who are a little too off-kilter to make it in a staid corporate environment.

---

* The names were usually based on something about you. So, for example, Donald Trump was Tower. Hillary Clinton was Everest (since Sir Edmund Hillary was the first to scale Mount Everest). Rudy Giuliani got Eagle (since he soared above us as StarQuest's boss). There was a local TV reporter named Dean Meminger whose dad played for the Knicks and was nicknamed "The Dream." Dean's Parks name? The Nightmare. My friend Paul LeBlanc was first named Whitey, but upon protest, got it changed to Pablo. Mine was Ivory.

The lessons of Parks and Henry were clear: Never underestimate your ability to move a politician if they believe you can move the media for or against them. If you can control the flow of attention, you can get people to do (or not do) quite a few things. This lesson, perhaps more than any other, has shaped everything I've done ever since.

4

Three Yards and a Cloud of Dust: Press Mainly Comes from Hard Work

A roll of toilet paper got me a job in the U.S. Senate. To be fair, it wasn't just any roll of toilet paper. One of the hardest things to do in the entire Parks system is to maintain bathrooms. Between the potential for crime and violence, the needs of the homeless, and just all of the weird shit that happens in New York City every day, bathrooms in parks are virtually impossible to keep safe and clean. For decades, the city just stopped building them.

But in the negotiations to fund the renovation of East River Park, which borders the East River in Manhattan from Chinatown up through the East Village, the construction of a new bathroom was somehow included. This called for a celebration, which meant a ribbon cutting to open the new facility. But why cut a ribbon when we could mark the occasion appropriately? Hence, the fated roll of toilet paper was ceremoniously cut, celebrated, and well publicized, which left enough of an impression on Steven Rubenstein, a PR guru in New

York to moguls like George Steinbrenner and Rupert Murdoch, that when Chuck Schumer was looking for a new communications director, he recommended me.

Chuck had just won a Senate seat two years earlier, upsetting longtime incumbent Al D'Amato. Chuck was (and is) a career politician and an extremely good one. After graduating from Harvard College and Harvard Law School, he disappointed his Jewish mother by running for a seat in the New York State Assembly rather than taking a job at a prestigious law firm. (I could relate.) His approach to the campaign was both genius and slightly crazy—he knocked on the doors of virtually every single voter in the district. And for a seat that couldn't matter less to 99 percent of voters, voting for the earnest young man who took the time to come see them was a reasonable choice. He repeated the same process a few years later to win a seat in the House (although now mainly substituting personal contact with omnipresent media coverage), and then again in 1998 to join the Senate.

If Chuck were a football player, he'd be a running back who plows straight ahead on almost every play. Three yards and a cloud of dust. But his intense work ethic and his incredible drive and instincts meant holding ceaseless press conferences on every topic imaginable (like the high price of breakfast cereal) to show New Yorkers he was working hard. Chuck understood that most voters don't really know what legislators do all day, but if the first thought that pops into their minds is "hard worker," that'd be enough for most of them. And since winning that moniker also meant Chuck could satisfy his favorite pastime—getting attention—it meant almost the entire Schumer operation revolved around getting press all day, every day.

The centerpiece of Chuck's week was the Sunday press conference. It had all the markings of what made Chuck successful—he was willing to work every Sunday when his peers were not, Sunday night's local newscasts were the highest rated of the week, and Monday's papers were usually starved for news, so whatever nonsense you made up on Sunday had a decent chance of getting a story on Monday.

Since Chuck, at the time, had very little actual power or authority (he was then just a junior senator whose party was in the minority, unlike now, where he's the most powerful Democrat in Washington), we'd have to invent stuff to get attention—naming a blue-ribbon commission to study the perils of tooth decay or writing a letter to the Ford Motor Company to protest the rising cost of windshield wiper fluid. And if the press couldn't make it to his event, no problem—he'd go to them. Once the TV stations figured out that they could just have Chuck come to the studio and re-create the press conference for them, we started spending half the day traveling around Manhattan, reading the same remarks for the TV cameras over and over again.

I usually started figuring out the Sunday press early in the week, but one week, I was at a total loss. The 2000 presidential election was in a few days. Chuck wasn't on the ballot, so we didn't have much to do. Bush-Gore was going to be close and everyone was hyperfocused on it, so a press conference about the need for better workplace protections for glass blowers wasn't going to get us much coverage.

New York still used antiquated voting machines—the kind where you pulled an actual lever for your candidate. They constantly broke, the lines to use them stretched around the block, and since we were in the midst of the dot.com boom, I figured there had to be new technology to make the experience better. So that Sunday's press conference unveiled the Schumer proposal to modernize America's voting system. We did fine—a few TV hits, a few small articles the next day—nothing special.

Two days later, the phrase "hanging chads" entered our lives. The system didn't work. We didn't even know who'd won the presidency. (Gore had gone so far as to concede to Bush and then retract his concession.) Someone was to blame. And we needed a new system—ASAP. Guess who had just proposed one?

A monsoon of press followed. Virtually every national broadcast and cable TV outlet, every newspaper, every magazine, and every radio station wanted to talk to Chuck about his voting reform proposal. Chuck was the expert, after all. He'd been talking about this a full two days before it became a national crisis. Our proposal turned into legislation and every step in the process—unveiling the bill, introducing the bill, getting a House sponsor, getting support from across the aisle, introduction into committee, committee hearings, and so on—was another chance for more press. Chuck was suddenly very happy with me and that gave me the confidence to channel my inner StarQuest and start coming up with newsworthy press conferences all week long (and at least twice on Sundays).

But the good times didn't last. Because the same election that brought us national attention on voting reform also brought Chuck's worst nightmare into the Senate: Hillary Clinton. As everyone knows, Hillary went from the Clinton White House straight to New York to run for the Senate.

While most states would reject a carpetbagger, New York had a tradition of electing outsiders. (Bobby Kennedy to the U.S. Senate in 1964; even Mike Bloomberg was originally from Massachusetts.) As New Yorkers, our inherent attitude is, "Of course everyone wants to be a New Yorker. Who wouldn't?"

The party paved the way for her nomination, no formidable Republican stepped up to challenge her, and she coasted into the Senate, technically as New York's junior U.S. senator (Pat Moynihan had just retired, making Chuck the state's senior senator) but also as the most famous person in Congress.

Having someone enter the Senate from your own state who could get more press by using the wrong elevator than you could get with fifty Sunday press conferences combined was the worst thing that could happen. Chuck didn't take it well.

5

When Things Go Truly Haywire, Seek Consensus

Over time—meaning over a very long time—Chuck and Hillary learned to appreciate each other. Despite Chuck's resentment at Hillary being handed something he'd worked his whole life to achieve, once they truly got to know each other, they had a lot in common. They were both very, very smart. Both were very hardworking. Both were exceptionally ambitious. Both were relatively centrist, except when the polling told them to pivot left or right. And while their motivations were complicated and by no means completely pure, they both genuinely believed in the power of government to help people. But at first, they hated each other.

In fairness to Hillary and her team, they probably didn't come into the Senate hating Chuck. He was one of many. She was her. But after spending nearly twenty-plus years scratching and clawing to get to the Senate, two fund-raisers and three press conferences at a time, Chuck had finally made it. And being the senior U.S. senator from

New York meant you could get as much attention as you wanted. Unless the junior senator also happened to be the most famous woman in the world.

Since nothing important actually happens in the Senate most days, the two offices stumbled along for most of 2001, warily circling each other like heavyweight boxers, with Chuck occasionally jabbing and Hillary mostly wanting him to just go away. We proposed meaningless ideas to get press every day.* Hillary endeared herself to old white male senators like Harry Byrd and John McCain to try to build a bipartisan narrative and track record.

Then came 9/11. In many ways, everything changed. And in some ways, nothing changed at all. On September 10, we had held a press conference on Long Island about a nursing shortage. Chuck headed back to D.C. that night. My plan was to stay in New York to make sure *Newsday* covered the story and then head back to D.C. the next afternoon.

I was sitting in our New York office. A news report flashed across the TV screen saying a small plane had crashed into the World Trade Center. It didn't seem like a major problem at the moment. I called Chuck to make sure he'd heard about it; he told me to keep an eye on it and went into his next meeting.

Minutes later, it became clear what had happened. I called Chuck back. He already knew. There was a tone in his voice I'd never heard

---

* In fact, since the entire point of a Sunday press conference was solely to get attention, there were times when our press hit was to send a letter to some corporation protesting something and use the press conference to announce the letter. We knew whomever we were attacking wouldn't be working that day, so they'd muster a weak response at best and we'd control the narrative. However, I started to notice that more and more of the responses were "We never received a letter." They were right—actually communicating with them was so beside the point, I'd literally forgotten to actually send them our letter of protest. Once the story came and went, I was onto the next one. It got so bad, I had to attach a Post-it note to my computer monitor saying, "Remember to send the letter."

before. Anger, rage, annoyance, and enthusiasm were all standard fare for him. This one was just shock. I called Harper at her office at MoMA. She hadn't heard yet. I started listing who'd been attacked—the World Trade Center, the Pentagon—and broke down by the time I finished the list at the White House. She was too stunned to even react.

The NYPD told us to evacuate the office. (A lady in the elevator yelled at us that having Chuck's office in the building made all the tenants a target and we should never come back.) Even though the warning signs were clearly there (the bombing of the USS *Cole,* the attempted bombing of the World Trade Center), until that moment, it still felt like we were completely safe, even invulnerable. Not anymore.

I didn't know what to do with myself once we left the building. I found myself standing on Third Avenue, looking north and south, unsure what to do or where to go. Finally, I walked over to my parents' apartment about ten blocks away and tried to work from there, but that day, running comms for a senator didn't offer much value to anyone, even to Chuck (who, to his credit, was laser-focused on the people he knew who were impacted directly by the tragedy; I couldn't even confirm whether he was available to appear on *Meet the Press*). I spent most of the day watching TV like everyone else. It was surreal to be watching what was happening and being in the place it was happening at the exact same time.

The next morning, Chuck and Hillary took a military plane back to the city and we joined a long procession including President Bush to visit Ground Zero. I had never seen anything like it. There were well over a hundred armed vehicles in the motorcade. There were F-16s patrolling from above. There were Army snipers positioned on the roofs of buildings all over Lower Manhattan.

We entered the secure perimeter, and because we were just twenty-four hours removed from the attack, it was as if Lower Manhattan had been frozen still at a moment in time. We passed a coffee cart completely flipped over but otherwise still intact. The debris and particles that would pollute Manhattan's air for months to come were already circulating, floating around our heads. Despite the presence of the president, the mayor, the governor, both senators, and so many other typically loud people, it was eerily quiet.

Once we entered Ground Zero, I lost sight of Chuck. For once, it didn't actually matter. We weren't the show that day. We were just there to listen and to help. The president started speaking, and to my surprise, I found myself standing about fifteen feet from him. I didn't vote for him in either election, but at that moment, he was as electric and powerful as any leader I've ever seen. He soon scrambled on top of a firetruck, issued his warning to Osama bin Laden, promised revenge, and told the cheering crowd that the whole world would hear from us soon. Even though much of the war that followed was extremely tragic, at that moment, George W. Bush was firmly in charge. It didn't matter that Bush was a Republican and we were Democrats, or that we disagreed on almost every issue. He was our president, and at least then and there, it felt right.

That afternoon, Bush flew back to D.C., but everyone else—Chuck and Hillary, Giuliani, George Pataki, Joe Allbaugh (the head of FEMA), all of the mayoral candidates (September 11 was supposed to be the mayoral primary), the city's entire congressional delegation, and half of the city commissioners—assembled at the Police Academy building on 20th Street to discuss next steps.

Republican mayor. Republican governor. Democratic senators. For once, it didn't matter. Giuliani ran the group through topics like how many body bags were needed, blood donation rates, and how we find and talk to family members of the victims—topics as serious as it gets. The sight of Hillary Clinton and Chuck Schumer diligently taking notes as Giuliani gave everyone orders spoke more to true bipartisanship than every panel, speech, book, and conference about how the two parties should work together combined.

Securing immediate federal aid to help New York City was the primary task given to the congressional delegation, and Chuck and Hillary quickly plotted strategy. Eventually, Chuck told us he was going to ask Bush for $20 billion.

"Why $20 billion?" I asked.

"It's the biggest number I can ask for without being embarrassed," he replied.

Since Bush was going to say yes to anything at that moment, luckily for New York, Chuck's natural aggressiveness meant he could ask for what seemed like an astronomical sum (at the time) with a straight face. This ended up being a really useful lesson: Always ask for as much as you can. That's true whether you're trying to help New York City recover from a terrorist attack or negotiating your salary for a new job, or if you're a startup founder negotiating your company's valuation with venture capitalists. The worst that happens is they say no and you retreat. But more often than you'd think, they say yes. The less shame you have, the better.

For a solid month, everyone played well in the sandbox together. While I initially questioned Chuck's need to be at every 9/11-related event and to convert everything 9/11-related into a media opportunity, it also didn't take long to realize that in this particular case, people really wanted their leaders to be visible. We New Yorkers like to think of ourselves as unflappable, but that wasn't true in the months following 9/11. Chuck was visible everywhere, all of the time. And to my surprise, it genuinely seemed to make everyone feel a little better. Until Frank Bruni came along.

6

Pick Your Narrative
Before Someone Else Does

When you're on the inside in politics, you frequently live in this fantasy world where you think you're calling the shots and controlling the agenda. And then every so often, the world harshly reminds you that you have a lot less control than you think. That reminder came in the form of a call from Frank Bruni.

At the time, Frank had been covering the Bush White House for the *New York Times*. He was assigned by the *Times* to write a cover story for their Sunday-supplement magazine about Chuck and Hillary's relationship—not a good topic for us.

While Chuck's and Hillary's disdain for each other was an open secret in Washington, this was still a full decade before the explosion of Twitter and Instagram, where every rumor, thought, meeting, and grudge is now disclosed to the world in real time. Senators from the same party and the same state rarely get along, so in normal times, a strained relationship wouldn't have been worth reporting on.

But in this case, we were just a month removed from the worst terrorist attack in U.S. history. New Yorkers wanted—even needed—to know that their leaders could put aside their personal and political differences and work together to help the city recover. Chuck understood that. Hillary understood that. Both staffs understood that. But Frank was (and still is) a great reporter. It wouldn't take much digging to uncover the animosity that had existed since the day Hillary entered the Senate. And while we couldn't really hide the past, both offices agreed that if we cooperated as much as possible going forward, we could present a united front and hopefully the piece wouldn't be about the petty rivalry of two of the most ambitious people in Washington.

We needed a foil—a better villain for the *Times* than each other. Thankfully, the Republicans came through. When Chuck and Hillary asked Bush for $20 billion in federal recovery aid for New York, he said yes on the spot. (Having just seen the carnage at Ground Zero, how could he not?) But Mitch Daniels, who, at the time, was the director of the federal Office of Management and Budget, hadn't discussed it with Bush beforehand and in no way wanted to part with $20 billion to help a bunch of liberal Democrats from New York.

Daniels had an ally in Trent Lott. Lott, the Senate minority leader at the time, was a good old Mississippi Republican who intuitively understood the value of the culture wars. For as long as his base saw their senators actively protecting their values from intrusions by gays, minorities, and anyone who seemed "ethnic," it didn't matter what kind of economic policies Lott and his colleagues pursued. That meant they could do Wall Street's bidding and keep the campaign cash flowing. Even though many of those policies didn't benefit the working-class whites who constituted their base, as long as Lott and his allies were keeping the outsiders at bay, they'd keep getting reelected.

Lott not only had no interest in giving New York $20 billion, but what could be better than staring down both the most hated woman by the Republican base and the politician who encompassed every New York stereotype with a heroic filibuster? And while no one could risk appearing unpatriotic right after 9/11, passing the Patriot Act and expressing support for military action against the aggressors (which ultimately led to the Iraq War) was more than enough cover. Lott could have his cake and eat it too.

For New York, this was a disaster. It was clear that $20 billion probably wouldn't begin to cover the cost of rebuilding, but it was a good start and firmly showed that the nation stood behind its largest, most important, and most controversial city. It also showed that the senators could get things done for their constituents. But none of that mattered to Lott. Which gave us an opening.

At this point, Hillary's press team and I were working together on an hourly basis to coordinate our response to Frank and keep him from focusing on the actual relationship of our respective bosses. Hillary was far more experienced in trying to divert attention from bad news, so she understood that no matter how she felt about Chuck at the time, demonstrating a fully united front to the *Times* was critical.

It was harder for Chuck. When the *Times* set up a photo shoot for the magazine's cover, Hillary had done enough of these to know to let the photographer just do his job. Chuck, despite having probably never snapped a photo in his life, of course knew better, telling the photographer he was doing it wrong. Chuck also tried to control what everyone said about him in the story. Frank asked me to respond to a few of the negative things people had said about Chuck. (It was nothing that we didn't all already know—all criticism of Chuck revolves around the same thing: his need for attention. It's his kryptonite since almost everything else about the guy—his work ethic, his intelligence, his savvy, his dedication—is impressive.)

I should have dismissed the criticisms as irrelevant and just let it go. Instead, I let Chuck know what people were saying in a fruitless attempt to get him to behave differently until the story came out. It backfired. Chuck picked up the phone immediately and called Joe Lhota, one of the critics Frank mentioned and who was, at the time, Giuliani's deputy mayor for operations, to complain bitterly. That only made things worse.

So now we had two dueling storylines—the easy one for Frank to write: that Chuck and Hillary couldn't get along, mainly because of Chuck's jealousy at the ease at which Hillary was able to get attention, or the far preferable one: that New York's two senators were working closely together to deliver for the city in the wake of the worst attack on U.S. soil since Pearl Harbor. Both stories were more or less true. One was prurient, insider, fun gossip, but seemed small and trivial in the context of the moment. The other was about the larger divide within the United States and whether or not we could overcome basic politics at one of the worst junctions in our nation's history.

Obviously, we pushed the latter narrative. Doing so was a variation on the old adage of answering the question you want to answer and not necessarily the question you're asked. If the partisan divide wasn't true, no amount of spin would have made a difference. (It would have been counterproductive.) But it was true and this was the time to rally behind New York. Lott and Daniels's opposition was repugnant to pretty much every New Yorker, and so luckily, Frank chose the latter narrative. (He hinted at the occasional tensions in the story but was basically kind to both senators.) And after facing immense pressure from the media, from Tom Daschle—the Senate majority leader—and from a White House that didn't really want to fund New York City but had no choice, Lott gave in and dropped his filibuster threat. New York got the money.

The story came out in mid-December and I was relieved. Both senators came off well—deeply concerned about New York, deeply committed to their constituents, and willing to do whatever it took to help the city get back on its feet (which all had the added benefit of being true). The story depicted their relationship as far better than it actually was. Chuck even came across as almost sanguine and accepting of his role as the senior senator who was far junior in stature and fame to his counterpart but still more than willing to do the hard work to serve his constituents.

He should have been thrilled. We'd avoided catastrophe, found a new narrative to replace the obvious one that would have made him look petty and small-minded, and instead helped him come off really good on the cover of the *New York Times Magazine* at a time when everyone was really paying attention.

He wasn't. Because the same day the story came out, Hillary did some event in Buffalo where he felt like she took credit for something he did.

"Did you see what she did?" he yelled.

I had no clue.

"That was our issue. My idea. She took credit for it. How did you let that happen?"

I was flabbergasted—not at the notion of a politician going somewhere and taking credit for something (she probably did do it and we would have too) but that after everything we'd just been through and everything we'd just achieved, he could even conceive of complaining.

"You guys need to work a lot harder."

That was the final straw. I lost it. All of the frustration of working for Chuck and all of the stress from living and working around the clock through 9/11 came out. I was working eighty hours a week and it'd seemingly gone unnoticed. Putting in those kinds of hours made me feel necessary and relevant, but my ego demanded at least a little recognition too (more than a little, to be honest).

I yelled. I screamed. I cursed. I stormed out of the office. Wouldn't take his calls. Told the staff I was gone for the day, if not for good. This, of course, terrified Chuck. Because whoever is running Chuck's press operation is like a crack dealer: He or she has what Chuck desperately needs and if that person decides to turn off the spigot, Chuck is like a junkie without a fix.

Eventually, I took his call. He apologized. I accepted. But I knew I had learned what I could learn working for Chuck. And I knew that spending my career mainly focused on getting someone attention for the sake of attention wasn't going to be enough to make me happy— even though leaving Chuck's office would mean an immediate downgrade in status, prestige, and influence.

This is a choice every young political staffer eventually faces, but it's more severe for those who work in communications. Because getting press is core to the needs of virtually every politician, a good press secretary can amass a lot of power, influence, and access at a very young age. But it becomes your skill set, and if you can't eventually pivot to something else, you'll likely end up spending your postgovernment career at a PR firm, never reaching anywhere near the heights you expected to when you were twenty-seven and advising a mayor or governor or senator. So, to me, the key was using a communications role to gain power and experience at a young age, but then to pivot away before it was too late. I finally found the pivot.

While we were busy trying to hide Chuck and Hillary's true relationship from Frank, Mike Bloomberg had just been elected mayor. As the Republican nominee, absent 9/11, Mike would have lost by twenty-five points. But the combination of the fear and shock everyone felt from the attacks; the desire for a strong, competent leader; the deification of Giuliani after he handled the response so well and his endorsement of Mike; the nasty, racially charged runoff between Mark Green and Fernando Ferrer, which depressed Democratic turnout in the general election*; the $72 million Mike spent on the campaign; and a very well-run operation by Mike's team was enough to (barely) put him over the top. New York City's mayor was now New York City's CEO.†

I had found my pivot, and I had an in. Ed Skyler, my closest friend—whom I had met at Parks—was Mike's press secretary in the campaign and had just been named city hall press secretary (both the youngest and tallest ever, and, in my view, the smartest). They were putting together an administration and Ed wanted me to join them. I did too. Because I had promised Chuck two years, I was on the hook for another eight months. But once 2002 started, I began running out the clock until my commitment to Chuck expired and I could come home, work on something other than someone's image, and, I hoped, work for the truly rare breed of politician who couldn't care less about politics.

In my mind, working for Mike meant working for one among the maybe 5 percent of politicians in total who truly get their job satisfaction by getting things done. I've found that this group, the rare breed, is one of the five you find in politics. The others are:

---

* Green's campaign darkened Ferrer's face in a flyer distributed on Staten Island, leading to outrage among Latino voters, many of whom retaliated by staying home on election day. The normal number of votes from Bronx Latinos that would have gone to the Democratic nominee was roughly also Bloomberg's margin of victory.

† One of Mike's best campaign ads made an issue of the racial strife during the Democratic primary. The spot featured a host of well-known New York Democrats talking about how race should never be used to divide people in campaigns. All of the quotes had come from other situations, but they applied to this situation too. One of the featured Democrats was Chuck. Terry McAuliffe, then the chairman of the Democratic National Committee, went ballistic that his own members were being used against the Democratic candidate for mayor. He called Chuck and demanded that Chuck tell Bloomberg to take the ad down. There was one problem: Chuck loved the ad. He looked great. He sounded great. His comment was spot-on. Bloomberg had put at least a million dollars behind the ad, so it was getting a ton of airtime. But it's hard to say no to the head of the party. So publicly, we issued a press release calling the ad misleading. But right before it went out, Chuck said to me, "Call your friend Skyler and tell him no matter what he reads and no matter what I say, leave the ad up." The day after the election, Chuck called Mike to congratulate him. Mike's response? "Thanks. And by the way, I just took your ad down."

- **The typical pol:** all the politicians out there who need the job to validate their insecurities. They're not inherently against accomplishments and they're not unwilling to do actual work—it's just secondary to their need for attention.*

- **The ideologue:** the true believer like the Green Party on the left or the Tea Party on the right. People like Bernie Sanders and Rand Paul are in this category.

- **The "I'm just happy to be here":** These are the backbenchers who do little or the people who only see their job as winning office, enjoying the perks and attention, and not actually governing.

- **The corrupt pol:** people constantly engaging in pay-to-play politics, trading donations for favors, and sometimes even taking outright bribes.

Some people cross into multiple categories but I have yet to meet anyone who can't be defined—and therefore understood and dealt with—by at least one of these criteria. Know which type of politician you're dealing with and knowing how to deal with them will be a lot clearer.

Of course, nothing is ever as easy as you think it will be before you actually go ahead and do it. So while working for a politician who fits squarely into the first category was a joy and a privilege, it came with its own set of challenges.

---

* Some people like Chuck fall into multiple categories. To deny he desperately covets attention and therefore belongs in the "typical pol" group would make this a work of fiction. But he's also in that 5 percent that does genuinely want to—and works hard to—get things done.

7

Subtlety Died Long Before Twitter

Even though he's now seen as New York City's most successful mayor, Mike Bloomberg's first year in office was rough. His proposal to ban smoking in the workplace was ultimately emulated both across the country and around the world, but when it first came up, it was reviled as a heavy-handed attempt to tell people what to do. His decision to raise property taxes to generate the revenue the city needed to fund the 9/11 recovery efforts was, of course, unpopular, as were some of the tough budget decisions he subsequently made, like closing extraneous fire houses. (You can imagine how well this went over just months after 9/11.)

Once I started working at city hall, it didn't take long to realize how professional and competent Mike and his team were, but it was just as easy to tell that the public clearly wasn't used to a nonpolitician in the mayor's office.* They were used to someone loud, aggressive, and in their face (Koch, Giuliani). That's not Mike. We knew that trying to make Mike something he wasn't—a typical pol—would ring false immediately. (Plus he'd never go for it.) But we needed something new to drive home who he was. Expecting the public—or even the media—to recognize he was different and create a new narrative for him wasn't realistic. We had to demonstrate it, visibly and tangibly. And it had to be radical enough to cut through all of the noise.

Mike's value proposition to voters is that he's uniquely competent, independent, apolitical, and honest. When I looked at our first year in office, it was clear to me that Mike wasn't going to get reelected based on his charm alone. We had to show the voters that he was so radically different from what they'd seen before—from what they were used to—that they were lucky to have him.

I started looking at what Mike promised in the campaign and comparing it to what he was doing as mayor. He was extremely active as mayor, but not many of his plans and policies stemmed from his campaign. And that's not a surprise—the job of running for office and the job of holding office are essentially two completely different roles. Candidates say what they have to say to win office. Most of them continue to do whatever's necessary to win reelection while they're in office. But Mike governed as if his first term were his last. And his greatest strengths—hiring and management—meant he brought in

---

* My first job for Mike was as co–executive director of the New York City Charter Revision Commission, which is a fancy way of saying that we ran a campaign to reform the city charter. We changed the line of succession to ensure a special election if the mayor has to step down for any reason—the charter previously gave the rest of the term to the public advocate, which is like making your idiot brother-in-law mayor—and the voters approved it overwhelmingly. No mayor has actually had to step down since so it's not a major accomplishment, but the win gave me the internal credibility at city hall to propose the next idea.

the most talented, creative, politically-independent people he could find from all over the country to run each city agency. They were interested in their own ideas, their own agenda—not what the campaign had proposed. All of that meant what happened in the election was ancient history.

But what if we could tie the two together to show that Mike was uniquely accountable and uniquely transparent? I started looking for examples of politicians who held themselves publicly accountable for completing their campaign promises. I couldn't find any. I then started researching what Mike promised during the campaign. He had hired smart policy experts like NYU's Mitchell Moss and Columbia's Esther Fuchs to run his policy operation, so they produced a host of good ideas, both big and small—ideas worth pursuing.

In fact, once I finished combing through every campaign press release, every newspaper article, the transcripts of every speech and debate, every campaign ad, and anything else I could find, it turned out they produced over three hundred and eighty different policy ideas. I put them all into a spreadsheet, went to Mike and his top staff, and proposed something I figured they'd probably hate: Let's become the first public official in history to publicly report on the status of every single campaign promise, regardless of whether it'd been fulfilled or not. If we'd fulfilled the promise, we'd say so. If we were working on it, we'd say where it stood. If we'd failed, we'd own up to it. And if Mike changed his mind on a particular issue, we'd explain why.

To me, it didn't really matter how many promises we actually fulfilled. The act of such radical transparency and accountability might be enough to get people thinking differently about Mike. Any other politician would have thrown me out of their office. (In fact, any politician other than Mike would have had an actual office—he sat in the bullpen with everyone else.) So of course, he loved it.

I started meeting with each commissioner to ask, "So how are you doing on these fourteen promises?" No one knew what I was talking about. Of course they didn't. That was the point. I explained what we were doing, why we were doing it, and that we were going to publicly report on the status of each promise in about six months, regardless of where each stood.

Most of them weren't thrilled. These weren't their ideas or vision. And they didn't want to risk embarrassment if their agency had the lowest completion rate. Some commissioners argued for policy changes to the promises, which I'd take back to Mike. Sometimes he agreed, sometimes he didn't. But before long, the agencies started reporting their progress, the campaign promises database took shape, and we started planning the unveiling. (The pressure of a specific announcement date was critical to ensuring the commissioners took it seriously.) We knew immediately with whom we wanted to unveil it.

Anthony Santamaria wasn't a typical Bloomberg voter. In fact, other than some rich people on the Upper East Side, there were no typical Bloomberg voters. But when Mike went to Bensonhurst, Brooklyn, in 2001 for a campaign event, Santamaria approached Mike and said, "You politicians are all the same. You come out here when you need our votes and then you never come back." Mike responded with a challenge and a promise: "Win or lose, I'll meet you at this same spot at 8 a.m. the day after the election."

Then 9/11 happened, Giuliani became a living legend and endorsed Mike, the Democratic candidates all imploded, and Mike actually won. And at 8 a.m. the next morning, Mike showed up at the D train station entrance at 79th and New Utrecht as promised (as did Anthony Santamaria).

Returning to Bensonhurst to become the first public official ever to report on the status of each and every campaign promise was a no-brainer.* Chris Coffey from Mike's advance team (Chris is now one of my partners at Tusk Ventures) tracked down Santamaria, and he agreed to join Mike that February for the unveiling of the campaign promises report. While I was excited to see what initially seemed like a crazy concept turn into reality, I also knew its culmination meant I'd need to figure out a new project at city hall. And then the phone rang.

---

* The *Times* did a fairly extensive analysis to figure out if Mike really was the first politician to ever do this. It turned out he was.

Not Being Qualified for a Job Shouldn't Stop You

How'd you like to be deputy governor of Illinois?"

"What's a deputy governor and why are you calling me?"

Although my reaction bordered somewhere between confusion, surprise, and suspicion that the call was meant for someone else, the lessons of getting the job for Rendell by wandering into city hall, of Chuck getting the $20 billion for New York City by having the balls to just ask for it, of convincing Mike to be the first politician to reveal the status of every campaign promise were clear: Nothing happens unless you make it happen. And even if all logic says that you're not qualified for something, that doesn't mean you don't take it anyway.

The call came from John Wyma. John and I had worked together in Chuck's office and we'd remained friends. Before becoming Chuck's chief of staff, John had performed the same role for a backbench congressman from Chicago named Rod Blagojevich. When Rod ran for governor of Illinois in 2002, John helped run the campaign. Rod wasn't the frontrunner. But his innate political skills were so superior, his fund-raising so good, and his campaign ads so effective that he shocked everyone by upsetting Chicago Schools Superintendent Paul Vallas in the primary and then besting Attorney General Jim Ryan in the general.

Rod ran as a reformer because the previous governor—George Ryan—was the latest in a string of Illinois governors to face criminal prosecution for corruption and the voters had had enough. They wanted change. They wanted reform. And Rod promised to give it to them.

It was an odd promise considering the source. Rod's career, until that point, had been anything but a paradigm of reform. His father-in-law, Dick Mell, was a Chicago alderman and ward boss, and used his influence to get Rod elected to the state legislature in Springfield. After four years of doing little in state government, opportunity struck. Dan Rostenkowski, the longtime congressman from Chicago's north side, was forced to resign in scandal after being caught writing personal checks on his government account. In the next election, a Republican—Mike Flanagan—managed to win the seat. But this was a Democratic district through and through and whoever won the nomination to oppose Flanagan next time around was guaranteed victory. Rod, although having accomplished literally nothing in his four years in the state legislature, had two things going for him: his innate political skills and his father-in-law.

In many ways, Rod exemplified the distinction between the skill set needed to run for office and the skill set needed to serve in office. Rod was an incredible public speaker. Charismatic. Charming. Funny. Self-deprecating. He could go into a black church, sing gospel—unironically—and bring the place down. He knew what you wanted to hear and had no qualms saying it, regardless of what it was or whether he actually meant it. He could shine in a speech to the state legislature, at a union hall, and in a TV ad. His retail political skills were better than anyone I'd ever seen (except maybe Bill Clinton) and when you combined that with his ward boss father-in-law's clout, beating more-qualified opponents to win the Democratic nomination to the House was within reach.

Parades with Rod especially were a lot of fun because he loved the crowd so much and they loved him. And no matter what direction you gave him, if there was a photo to take with someone, he took it. If there was a hand to shake, he shook it. If there was a baby to kiss, he kissed it. Even really basic precautionary instructions like "At the gay pride parade, don't pose for the TV cameras with the giant dildo" went unheeded. I liked that about him.*

And while Rod possessed none of the skills, work ethic, discipline, integrity, or focus to perform any real work once he won office, the task of getting there came easy to him.† Rod won the House seat and proceeded to spend the next six years as a backbencher, passing only one minor bill (naming a post office).

But he was ambitious. Some of it probably came from the same insecurity that drives most politicians—the need for attention, the need for affirmation, the need for validation. Some of it came from the chip on his shoulder of being a first-generation American and wanting to show that he belonged and that all of the sacrifices everyone made to get to this country and put him in a position to succeed were worth it. (I could relate, having had the same expectations pressed upon me at

---

* Rod also had something that some politicians do and some just don't: the vote-getting gene. Either you're born with it or you're not. And it's not solely based on charisma or looks—it's more intrinsic than that. Bill Clinton had it. Hillary Clinton does not. George W. Bush had it. His father and brother did not. Rod had it in spades. If you're trying to analyze an election, once you've covered all the obvious stuff, look at whether the candidate has that vote-getting gene and whether the candidate fits the zeitgeist of that moment. In my experience, the answers to those two questions will tell you more about the outcome than a dozen different polls ever could.

† In fact, Rod never lost a race in his entire career. He won two state legislative races, three congressional races, a massive upset to become governor, and then a double-digit victory to capture a second term.

every turn throughout my childhood.)* And despite having no real ideology, no real policy goals, no interest in governance, and certainly no
real interest in reform, in 2002, Rod launched a campaign for governor.

By all rights, he shouldn't have won. He wasn't qualified. He had
few—if any—accomplishments to point to. He didn't have any ideas
that rallied people around him. But he was exciting. He was a brilliant
fund-raiser. And he hired a very talented guy named Bill Knapp to
make a series of TV ads that personified him as the American Dream.
(People would recite the opening line to me even years later: "My name
is Eastern European but my story is American.") As we all know, Rod
won. And like Robert Redford in *The Candidate,* he pretty much looked
at his campaign team and said, "What do we do now?"

His first choice for deputy governor—a very smart and decent guy
named Doug Scofield—lasted only a few weeks. Doug was a reasonable adult and thought he was entering a job that would give him the
chance to set a new direction for the state of Illinois. But working for
Rod wasn't something that any reasonable adult would endure. And so
a month after the inauguration—as I was sitting in city hall in New
York putting the final touches on the campaign promises report—I
was asked to fly to Chicago and meet Rod.

Why me? I've asked myself that question a lot over the years. It's been
asked of me by reporters, legislators, prosecutors, pundits, business leaders, clergy—and anyone too polite to ask it directly was certainly wondering it. I was twenty-nine years old. Other than having gone to law
school in Chicago, I had no connection to Illinois. I didn't know Rod (I'd
met him once in D.C. at dinner with John Wyma a few years earlier) and

---

* Rod and I had a lot of differences, but we were both always on the lookout for slights, we both
always relished a fight, and we both understood that you could curse and scream at each other one
moment and be totally back to normal the next. Ironically, that trait allowed me to fight with him
constantly—and tell him what an idiot he was—and that willingness to say no and take the
stream of invectives it produced ended up keeping me out of trouble.

hadn't worked on his campaign. So why turn over the operations of the nation's fifth-largest state to a total stranger? It wasn't like a job at city hall in New York, which had half a dozen deputy mayors at any given time. There was just one deputy governor. The job encompassed everything: operations, budget, policy, legislation, communications—far and away the most powerful unelected position in the state. And when news eventually hit that I'd been appointed, everyone in Illinois politics scratched their heads.

As far as I can tell, there are two explanations for why I got the job: one benign and one less so. The benign one goes something like this: I was young and being deputy governor was a career-making job for me. That meant I'd be willing to tolerate a lot of nonsense from Rod that any rational adult wouldn't. I also knew a little bit about a lot of different things: policy from my time at city hall, communications from my time in the Senate, operations from my time at Parks. I had good names on my résumé: Bloomberg, Schumer, Rendell, University of Chicago, Penn. But that only tells part of the story.

The less-benign explanation wasn't clear to me until seven years later when I read the indictment of Rod and the others arrested with him. I was still a naïve kid. I didn't understand the cesspool of Illinois politics. I didn't know the players. And in retrospect, a few things were conspicuously absent from my job portfolio: hiring, grants, and contracts. To me, those all seemed like uninteresting administrative burdens, so I was happy to let someone else handle them. But if you're looking to execute a massive pay-to-play scheme—auctioning off jobs, contracts, and grants to the biggest campaign donors—it's all you care about. Rod and his cronies figured they could do what they wanted—and let me worry about running the state—and I'd never notice. And other than the one time Rod slipped up and asked me to extort Rahm Emanuel, they were right.

I flew out to Chicago over Presidents' Day weekend. We met in Rod's office in the Thompson Center (the main state office building in Chicago). In addition to Rod, John was there, as was Lon Monk—Rod's campaign manager and chief of staff—and Chris Kelly, his lead fundraiser, close friend, and, ultimately, the guy whose sloppiness and greed helped bring the whole thing crashing down.*

Deputy governor seemed like a pretty big job to me, so I did my homework. I used LexisNexis to download every story I could find, read it all carefully, and wrote up some notes that gave me passing familiarity with most of the issues. Knowing at some point, he'd say to me "Any questions?" I wrote up around a dozen of them.

In retrospect, it should have been a red flag that my preparation impressed him so much. Sure, I'd put some work in, but it wasn't particularly extensive or novel. It was just basic blocking and tackling. But to Rod, it was as if I'd memorized the entire contents of the Bible and recited it back in haiku in twelve different languages.

As luck would have it, a massive snowstorm hit Chicago and I was stuck there a few extra days. That gave me more time to try to impress Rod and the team and it must have worked, because I flew home with the job in hand. I still wasn't even sure I should take it.

The Bloomberg city hall was just a giant bullpen where everyone sat in one big room. John Crotty, who ran the city council lobbying efforts for Mike, sat next to me and we'd become friends (still are). I pulled him into the Staten Island room. (Each conference room was named for a borough.)

"What are you, nuts? Of course you have to do it."

"I'm twenty-nine. I'm a New Yorker. I've never even worked in state government. And I know nothing about Illinois."

---

* When it all went bad, Rod went to jail, Lon went to jail, and Chris killed himself. John had cooperated and given the prosecution the probable cause they needed to wiretap Rod's phones.

"Look, someone gives you an opportunity like this, you take it. Period. Once you do a job like this, you're gonna have great opportunities for the rest of your life. It's like NFL coaches. Once you're a head coach somewhere, you always end up getting another job somewhere else. Even if you suck."

"Hopefully I won't suck."

"Don't get ahead of yourself." He stood up, smiled, clapped me on the back, and went back to the bullpen.

We launched the campaign promises report later that week, and I told Mike I was moving on. I'd been warned that once you tell him you're leaving, you're basically dead to him and can never come back. I'd only been at city hall for a little over six months and in that time, he'd given me a lot of responsibility and freedom. And here I was, walking away. So I was nervous.

He seemed surprised when I told him. "Deputy governor? Really?" If it hadn't seemed almost as implausible to me, I might have taken offense. But once he was clear what my new job was, what else was he going to say? Stay here and be one of fifty people running city hall when you can go be the sole person running a big state? So he stuck out his hand, wished me the best, and told me not to fuck it up.

The press reception in Illinois when they announced my appointment wasn't quite as gracious. Chicago calls itself the Second City for a reason. They see themselves as a rival of New York City, and while they won't go as far as to argue the two cities are equivalents, they see it as a close call. Of course, not a single New Yorker feels any rivalry with Chicago whatsoever. (Whenever someone would visit us from New York, their reaction was always pleasant surprise, not because they had low expectations of Chicago, but because what Chicago was like had never once crossed their minds.) The same jealousy and insecurity that Chicagoans feel toward New York applies to the rest of Illinois, but the target of their angst is Chicago. (The Peoria paper would literally call him "Rod Chicagovich.") So when news broke that a twenty-nine-year-old New Yorker with no real connections to Illinois was coming in to run the entire state, the press and the political chattering class were divided between confused, offended, and outraged.*

If I'd been older, wiser, more mature, and more experienced, I probably would have read the coverage, seen the whole thing as a bad idea, realized how much I enjoyed my life in New York, and stayed home.

But that same naiveté that made me appealing to Team Blagojevich also meant I didn't know that I wasn't supposed to be able to just walk into a brand-new environment, start telling everyone what to do, and that it'd somehow work out. And sometimes what you don't know can't hurt you.

---

* Although the political cartoon of Rod driving a car and me sitting next to him in a car seat was kind of funny.

9

People Want to Be Led

stuck my head in the conference room, panicked, and jumped back into the hallway. It was the day of the budget address—we were unveiling our plan to eliminate a $4.8 billion deficit and I'd worked around the clock with John Filan, our budget director, since I'd landed at Midway a few weeks earlier to figure out a way to close the gap and fund the government without raising taxes or cutting spending for education, health care, or public safety.*

Truth is, I had no idea how to compile a state budget. I just made it up as I went along, using whatever common sense I had, whatever information I could gather, and just working really, really hard. (Luckily

---

* I should have known it was a bad omen when I landed in Chicago, went to get my luggage, and my garment bag had burst open. My suits from Century 21 were each rotating around and around on the luggage belt. I probably should have just collected them and gotten on the next flight back to New York.

my office had a couch because sleeping on the floor would have been pretty uncomfortable.) When I look at most startup founders now, I find myself wondering if they really know what they're doing too. But then I remember my time in Illinois and figure if they have the chutzpah, work ethic, and creativity, there's no reason they can't succeed.

I hadn't met most of the directors of the state agencies yet. I didn't even know most of their names—although they'd certainly read a lot about me in the past few weeks. I decided to assemble them before the speech to give them an overview of the budget and the fight ahead to pass it.

The first thought that crossed my mind when I stuck my head in the room was, *Holy shit. There are a lot of adults in there.* Suddenly, I wasn't the deputy governor or the former staffer for a U.S. senator or the mayor of New York City. I was the kid walking into the Democratic Convention in 1992, about eight hours removed from cleaning poop out of inflatable pools. *Just walk in there and tell them how it's gonna be,* my brain instructed my legs.

I entered the room, sat down at the head of the table, smiled, and introduced myself. They smiled back. And that was enough. As I walked through the budget, the reasoning behind it, and our odds of passing it, they were attentive, eager for information. It turned out, until that day, no one had ever bothered to assemble them. They were completely rudderless. So while a twenty-nine-year-old New Yorker might not have been their first choice to lead them, at least someone was finally doing it.

I learned quickly that most people really want someone else to be in charge and bear the responsibility for bad decisions. And even if you think they're far older, more experienced, and even more qualified than you are, if you take their calls, reply to their emails, show real interest in their work, and are willing to take responsibility and make decisions, they'll not only accept you, the vast majority of the time they'll gladly do whatever you tell them to do. And if you're willing to reject the notion that shit flows downhill and instead be the one protecting them from egos, politics, and personalities, they'll follow you anywhere.

That need for leadership proved far more acute over the next few months in two disturbing ways. The first was a phone call. I was at Rod's house one morning because Rod preferred to work from home. ("Work" meaning a loose mix of a few phone calls, watching *SportsCenter*, reading long biographies of Napoleon, preparing to go for a run, going for a run, stretching after the run, and then showering for at least ninety minutes after that.)

Rod was livid. His father-in-law, alderman and ward boss Dick Mell, had sent out a fund-raising letter. Politicians raise money—no surprise there. But Mell noted in the letter that the governor would be headlining the fund-raiser, which probably seemed natural to anyone reading it. But Rod apparently hadn't been told about it beforehand. Mell just did it. And while it'd seem like a minor oversight to you and me, to Rod, it was a clear sign that even though he'd just won the governorship of the fifth-biggest state in the nation, his father-in-law still saw him as a stooge who sang and danced when the strings were pulled.

Rod saw the letter and went fucking ballistic. Ranting and raving. Yelling and screaming. Shutting down the fund-raiser to show Mell who was boss was the only thing in the world that mattered. Which, on a normal day, would have been fine—it's not like Rod was busy running the state anyway. But this wasn't a normal day. I had gone over to Rod's house to make sure he joined a conference call with Homeland Security secretary Tom Ridge and eight other governors. Since we were only eighteen months removed from 9/11, tensions were still high. The federal government conducted a series of tabletop exercises to simulate everyone's roles during an actual terrorist attack.

Every few months, a group of governors would get on a call to walk through a drill, take in information, and make decisions like declaring a state of emergency and activating the National Guard. The call was in half an hour. Rod was on the other line, screaming at Chris Kelly to tell every donor to boycott Mell's event. The call was in twenty minutes. Rod had just ripped Mell's letter into a dozen pieces and thrown them down the stairs. The call was in ten minutes. Rod was downstairs somewhere, slamming doors. (Even though it was a little awkward to be left alone in his bedroom, it was far preferable to being within a ten-foot radius of him.)

I ventured downstairs, found him, and said, "Hey. We need to dial in to this call."

"What call?"

"What do you mean what call? The call with Tom Ridge. Why do you think I'm here?"

"I'm not doing it."

"Of course you're doing it. You have to. It's the secretary of the Department of Homeland Security. And, like, eight other governors. It's not optional."

He gave me a hard look. "You do it."

I looked at the clock on my BlackBerry. The call was in three minutes.

"I can't do it. It's for governors, not for staff."

"This is more important."

"Screaming about a fund-raising letter from an alderman is more important?"

"Yes."

The call was in two minutes.

"I can't. I'm not the governor. No one voted for me."

"Well, I'm not doing it." He walked out of the room.

It was 10:31. The call was starting. I dialed in.

My plan was to explain that there was an emergency and he couldn't make it. But they'd already started. Ridge was talking. And this wasn't an informal discussion. It was a planned military exercise. Ridge was outlining the simulated crisis and asking governors to declare a State of Emergency. He went through the states. Voices were saying yes.

"Governor Blagojevich?"

Shit. It would have been way too weird to first start explaining what had happened. And this was an emergency—albeit a simulated one. I deepened my voice a little, which didn't even really make sense since it wasn't like Rod's voice was deeper than mine in the first place.

"Governor Blagojevich?"

"Yes. I declare a state of emergency."

I don't remember the rest of the call that well. I was just relieved no one asked "Who is this?" when I spoke. I didn't need to speak again during the call, and when it ended, I looked around to tell Rod it had gone fine. I could hear him in the kitchen, screaming into the phone. He didn't see me. The coast was clear. I walked out the front door and drove back to the office. It was the first of many close escapes from the Blagojevich residence.

A few months later, we'd survived the legislative session, passed the budget, and were now deep into bill review. Bill review is a laborious process where you take every piece of legislation passed that session and analyze it from a policy, legal, and budgetary standpoint. Once that was done, I'd assemble the team, we'd review the pros and cons of each bill, and then I'd form a recommendation for Rod to sign or veto it. Typically, the legislature would pass around four hundred bills every session. The vast majority of them were meaningless—things like "the official state amphibian is the frog"—but around a hundred or so had meaningful public-policy implications. Each bill also has a timeline and if it's not acted upon within sixty days, it automatically becomes law.

I was in my office in the Thompson Center, overlooking the Chicago River. Rod didn't carry a cell phone so I called him at home. (He was almost always home so the lack of a cell phone wasn't that big of a problem.) While he had spent some time in Springfield during the legislative session to negotiate the budget, he'd been coming into the office less and less.

"Hey, listen. You need to come by the office. We're at the deadline to decide on a bunch of bills and I need you to decide what you want to do with them."

"I'm busy."

Doing what? I wondered, but kept it to myself. "Well, there are about twenty bills with deadlines in the next week. Maybe we can just go over those?"

"I have to go see Rocco today." Rocco was his tailor. Why the governor could only visit his tailor during business hours or why Rocco couldn't come to him or why having Rocco on the schedule meant he couldn't do anything else that day was unclear.

"Well, how about on the way to Rocco? Or the way back?"

"I'm picking out fabrics for three new suits. It's gonna take a while."

I got the message. While the twenty or so bills under consideration were all important, none were very controversial. And since Rod didn't pay attention to the inner workings of his administration, if our decisions weren't newsworthy, he wouldn't find out about it anyway. And even if he did weigh in on something that turned out to be the wrong call, he'd blame someone else, so there was almost no point in securing his buy-in.*

---

* Take emergency contraception, for example. Some pharmacists in Illinois were refusing to fill prescriptions for emergency contraception and we issued an executive order prohibiting this practice. Not surprisingly, this was very popular on the Left. So when *The Daily Show* called wanting to do a segment on the issue, we were happy to make Rod available. Rod was a funny guy and was the hero in this case. Except we made one key mistake: We assumed Rod knew it was a comedy show. It only became clear he didn't when he started being asked crazy questions by the correspondent and got more and more flustered with each one (which meant instead of the segment mocking right-wing pharmacists, it ended up mocking Rod). Rod managed to make matters even

"So what do you want to do?" I asked.

"You do it. I'm too busy."

When I testified in Rod's first corruption trial seven years later, someone went back to see if the four years of legislation I'd either signed or vetoed were even valid. Because we used the autopen, they were.

Sometimes I'd go with him to Rocco if I felt like whatever decision I'd made was going to be controversial and I at least wanted Rod's buy-in before I did it. (Not that it spared me a tongue lashing if the decision then got bad press; to Rod, perception and reality were almost flipped—the substance mattered little to him and the perception was critical, regardless of the merits of the issue at hand—in other words, it was the perfectly logical response from someone who only saw his job as winning office and preparing to win it again in four years.)

During that first summer, the main thought flashing through my mind was, *Holy shit. We just moved halfway across the country to work for a guy who literally won't even come to the office. What am I going to do?**

Then we completed the bill review process. It was time to start thinking about the next year's budget and legislative agenda. The best part about working in government, far and away, is that you can come up with an idea at breakfast, and if you have the power or talent to enforce it or sell it, it can be public policy by lunch. And in a big state like Illinois, it can impact millions of people. It's both a big responsibility and a big opportunity. (One I'm not sure I had the maturity to fully appreciate during my time there.)

---

worse a few weeks later when he blamed his performance on his staff for not properly briefing him. In this case, he was actually right, but because Rod never took responsibility for anything, at that point, he was the boy who cried wolf and his finger pointing only made the ridicule even worse—although still not as bad as the time he used the phrase "testicular fortitude" when speaking in front of a classroom of third graders.

* I asked Lon one day if Rod could work harder. Lon had been Rod's roommate in law school before running his campaign and becoming chief of staff. He just laughed.

We started kicking around new policy ideas. The state's schools were run by an independent agency who did little to demand accountability or results. What if we pushed for gubernatorial control of schools? New technology was emerging that could make it a lot easier to collect tolls without requiring a car to stop or even slow down. What if we tore down all the tollbooths across the Illinois Tollway system and replaced them with Open Road Tolling? There were hundreds of thousands of kids in Illinois without health insurance. What if we found a way to cover them?

And then it hit me. I'd been looking at it all wrong. The right thought wasn't, *Holy shit, the governor is totally MIA.*

The right thought was, *Holy shit, this guy is totally checked out. Someone's gotta run the place. And if no one's going to tell us what we can and can't do, we might as well do as much as we can.*

And we did, to the great frustration of everyone in the Illinois political firmament who liked things the way they were. While Rod never became any easier to deal with, I did my thing (running the state), he did his thing (going for long runs), and it worked reasonably well. Until it didn't.

10

It's All Fun and Games
Until Someone Goes to Jail

Where the fuck is the money?"

I didn't know what Rahm was talking about, but that wasn't unusual for our conversations. Neither was being cursed at or hung up on. (It was all somewhere between par for the course and a badge of honor.)

"Which money for which thing?" I asked.

"The two million. For the school. In my district. Rod promised them the money a year ago. And he's still jerking them around. I've fucking had it with you guys." At the time, Rahm Emanuel was a congressman representing the northwest side of Chicago.

I still didn't know what he was talking about, so I promised to look into it and get back to him. Later that day, I asked John Harris, Rod's chief of staff at the time, about the grant. (John oversaw grants as well as contracts and hiring.)

"That's a Rod thing. Above my pay grade," he replied.

That night, Rod and I were on the phone about whatever PR crisis we were facing that day.

"I meant to tell you, Rahm's really upset."

He laughed. "What else is new?"

"I know, but this was about something specific. He was asking about money for an athletic field for a school in his district. Said you promised it a long time ago."

Rod was silent for a moment. "That's not happening right now," he finally said.

"Why not?" It was a stupid question because the answer led to me having to testify in both of Rod's federal corruption trials.

"Because he owes me a fund-raiser. His brother promised to host one a long time ago. It hasn't happened." Rahm's brother is Ari Emanuel, the legendary Hollywood mogul.

"What does that have to do with the grant?"

He got annoyed. "Because if we release the grant, then Rahm doesn't need anything from me. And then the fund-raiser will never happen."

I didn't say anything. I should have said, "No—you can't connect the two." But that was obvious. It wasn't that Rod didn't know the rules. He just didn't follow them.

"Tell Rahm he needs to get the fund-raiser done first," Rod told me. "Then we'll release the grant."

I wanted nothing to do with this conversation. Holding up a government grant to get a campaign fund-raiser was clearly unethical and illegal. I'm not sure why, after three and a half years of keeping me out of these types of conversations, Rod took a different direction that night. I wish he hadn't. I also couldn't believe he was that stupid—beyond the ethics and legality, Rahm was leading the Democratic effort to retake control of the House. He was a really smart, really powerful guy. Not someone to fuck with. I got off the phone as quickly as I could.

I took a deep breath and made two phone calls. The first was to John

Wyma. John was, at the time, close to both Rod and Rahm. John was also one of Rod's most prolific fund-raisers, and as a lobbyist, John desperately needed to be in Rod's good graces. I was worried that Rod would tell John what he told me and John would feel pressured to do it. John understood immediately that Rod's demand was nothing short of criminal and said he'd make sure he did nothing if Rod raised it with him.

Then I called Bill Quinlan, Rod's general counsel. "You need to get your client under control," I told him. I explained the conversation Rod and I had just had. Quinlan said he'd take care of it.

The grant was distributed, although John Harris—presumably at Rod's direction—meted it out in tiny increments so there was rarely any sense of comfort by the school that their project would be funded. (I guess Rod and John were still hoping for the fund-raiser.) The fund-raiser never happened. Rod was reelected by double digits that November. I left the following month, and never spoke to Rod again.

When Rod was arrested, attempted extortion of Congressman Emanuel was one of the charges. Of course, auctioning off Obama's Senate seat to the highest bidder got most of the attention (and is what led to Rod's conviction and fourteen-year prison sentence), but once I saw the indictment, I knew I'd be getting a call from the feds pretty soon.

The FBI reached out to me a few weeks later and asked me to explain what had happened.* I'm not sure whether the rantings of a

---

* I met with the FBI on January 31, 2009. They wanted me to come see them in Chicago, but Harper was very pregnant with our second child, Lyle, and it seemed too close to the due date to leave town. The night before my meeting, we had dinner and Harper said she thought Lyle could come early, just like our daughter, Abigail, had. The next morning, as I nervously got dressed for the meeting, Harper's water broke. She told me to go to the meeting since it'd probably be a while before it was time to go to the hospital. I got to the offices of Akin Gump, where my friend and lawyer, Rich Zabel, was hosting the meeting. I told him what had happened. The meeting began and while they kept assuring me I was just a witness and the good guy, I was still pretty terrified. Then my phone rang. It was Harper. The doctor wanted us to come to the hospital right away. "I gotta go," I told the team of prosecutors and agents assembled around the long conference room table. "What do you mean you have to go? We all flew out here for this." I shrugged. Rich talked to the lead prosecutor. I was excused from the meeting and Lyle was born later that day.

sociopath during a late-night phone call about something that never actually happened was criminal (and both juries apparently agreed, not convicting him on the charge in either trial), but thank god I didn't just acquiesce to what Rod wanted—or hang up and ignore the issue completely. By talking to his lawyer—who also served as the chief ethics officer for our office—I was able to prevent something very stupid from happening. And I was able to preserve my own freedom and reputation. It's never fun fighting with your boss, especially when you work for someone a little (well, maybe a lot) crazy like Rod Blagojevich. But the alternative was far, far worse.

11

Pick Your Enemies = Win Your Battles (Strangle the Baby in the Crib)

escaped Illinois with my freedom, but after working for a governor who'd become known for corruption, crazy hair, and being fired by Donald Trump on *Celebrity Apprentice,* I made a career choice that turned out to be almost as bad. I took a short-lived stint as an investment banker at Lehman Brothers just before they imploded the entire global economy.

Luckily, the day Lehman collapsed was the day I rejoined the Bloomberg team. Mike wanted to run for a third term and once the city council changed the term limits law to allow him to run again, he named me campaign manager.

The opportunity to work for Mike again was a gift. But the challenge at hand was far more daunting than anyone realized. So much so that the campaign was really a campaign to make sure no one knew that we could be beaten by a well-run campaign. In other words, we were vulnerable. Seventy percent of registered voters in New York City are Democrats. More than half of them are party-only voters, meaning they're going to vote for the Democratic candidate for any office no matter what.

For mayor, that meant the Democratic nominee—our opponent—would walk in with roughly 45 percent of the vote. And for us, that meant we had to win almost everyone else (which meant of the available 55 percent of votes, we had to win 90 percent of them). And that was before the 2008 election of President Obama had excited and energized Democratic voters.

To make matters worse, Mike had very publicly left the Republican party the year before, so he had insulted the most partisan of the roughly 12 percent of city voters who were Republicans. We were running in the middle of the worst financial crisis since the Great Depression, and while our argument was that only Mike could guide New York safely through it, there was a lot of antipathy toward billionaires in general. And because Mike governed without regard to politics, he'd made a lot of people angry over the years: frequently the same people whose votes he needed. While Mike never really had a political base, he relied on typical Giuliani supporters—white ethnic homeowners in Brooklyn, Queens, the Bronx, and Staten Island. And then he promptly raised their property taxes to help the city fund the 9/11 recovery efforts. He also raised their water rates. (The single greatest threat to the city was the lack of backup on its water supply, so building a third water tunnel was essential, but expensive.) He enforced parking tickets. They might have liked that the city felt clean and safe and that their local schools were improving, but this guy was costing them money, all of the time. Not a great way to win their support.

And then there were term limits. I knew it was a serious problem when we held a focus group of Latino voters not long after the bill passed to allow Mike to run for a third term.* Mike was popular with some Latino demographics (typically recent immigrants from Mexico, Central America, and parts of South America) and less so with others (typically Puerto Rican and Dominican voters). Not on this night. Virtually every topic came back to his decision to change the law on term limits. And even worse, it reminded many of them about everything they hated about their home country. (We heard some version of "I left because this was the kind of shit they pulled" time and again.) White liberals—whose votes we needed—felt similarly, and lots of other voters who liked Mike and probably would have voted for him absent the term limits controversy decided they'd just sit out the race.

We did the math. It wasn't good. Mike won 57 percent of the vote in 2005, which actually exceeded the ceiling for any non-Democrat. Now start subtracting: the Obama effect, being a billionaire in the recession, leaving the Republican party to become an Independent, property taxes, water bills, and, of course, term limits. It wasn't clear there was enough room to get to 50.1 percent.

What was clear was that our ability to squeak over the line depended on two factors: (1) our opponent, and (2) whether we could convince everyone with any electoral influence, money, or power (the Democratic party, Obama, the unions, the newspapers, clergy, local elected officials, local county parties, major Democratic donors, etc.) to stay out of the race. Because if they realized that they could win if they all banded together behind the right candidate, we'd be toast.

---

* Having run the process to change the term limits law, I knew what I was getting into.

Three or four leading local Democrats expressed interest in running against us. Bill Thompson, the city comptroller, was next in line and felt like it was his turn. Thompson was a product of the Brooklyn Democratic machine, eventually landing in the Office of the Comptroller, which was the second- or third-most-powerful job in city government, depending on how you look at it. Thompson was cautious, personally conservative, and very conventional. If he ran, he'd capture every traditional Democratic vote. But he wasn't exciting, he didn't work hard, and we knew what we were getting.

The wild card—and greatest threat—was a then-congressman from Brooklyn and Queens named Anthony Weiner. (Yep, same guy you saw in the tabloids every day for months on end.) Anthony was everything Thompson wasn't. Fiery. Loud. A constant stream of ideas. An even-more-constant need for attention. (It won't shock you to learn that Anthony worked in Schumer's office before beginning his own political career and modeled his approach on Chuck's.) He was a Jewish guy with an Italian first name. He came from white ethnic Queens but was (at the time) married to Huma Abedin, Hillary Clinton's top aide, and moved easily in the world of money and glamour. He was a great fund-raiser. He was tireless. He was a problem.

And on the math alone, he was even scarier: most black and Latino voters, who comprised about half the electorate at the time, were likely to stick with the Democratic candidate whoever it was. That we could live with. But Weiner was also going to be a far more appealing candidate to our core voters: Jews and Catholics. Remember, we needed 90 percent of the nonautomatic Democratic vote to win. Our margin for error was nonexistent.

Weiner had to be stopped before he started. Waiting and seeing was the worst thing we could do—it'd be making the same mistake that so many big companies commit when they ignore potential disruption from startups until it's too late. You have to pick your enemies whenever you can. You have to strangle the baby in the crib.*

Weiner had announced that he'd make a decision by Memorial Day, so we had a few months to run a mini-campaign to convince him not to run. We weren't going to get there with honey: We couldn't promise to support him in 2013, and since attention for the sake of attention was Anthony's main goal, the risk of going to him to try to cut a deal and having him blow it up in spectacular public fashion was too great.

So we had to make the risk of running so severe that he'd ultimately choose not to run. We started by reverse engineering his decision. Weiner's pollster was Joel Benenson (who had just won fame as Obama's pollster) and Joel had worked at the same firm as two of our pollsters, Doug Schoen and Bernard Whitman.

"It's fairly simple," Doug explained. "If he's announcing his decision by Memorial Day, that means they'll need to have polling results a few days before, so figure they go into the field about ten days before the announcement. I know how Joel thinks. If they're down by less than ten, he's telling Anthony to run. If they're down by more than fifteen, he's not running. And if it's between ten and fifteen, it'll be a close call." Bernard nodded in agreement.

It made our task pretty clear: we had to be up by fifteen or more by the time Joel went into the field.

A good campaign usually deploys multiple tactics: paid media (TV ads, digital ads, radio ads, print ads), earned media (which is

---

* One upside of Mike being so focused on governing and so uninterested in politics is we had the autonomy to make decisions on issues like shaping the playing field. He would have found—and did find—most of what we did to drive Anthony out of the race distasteful. But we made a point of doing what we felt we needed to do and then apologizing later if he saw it and yelled at us—not unlike the beg for forgiveness approach that governs much of our work for startups.

just jargon for public relations), opposition research (a euphemism for digging up dirt on someone), field (canvassing, door knocking, flyers, lit drops, posters, phone calls), lobbying (personal connections in one way or another), and today, perhaps more than anything else, social media. We went at it on every front. I convened a meeting of our senior team every morning at 8 a.m. to discuss what we could to do to drive Anthony from the race. Here's the best of what we did:

- **Earned media:** I kicked things off by saying, on the front page of the *New York Times,* that if Anthony ran, I'd add an extra $20 million to our campaign budget to ensure that we destroyed his reputation so thoroughly, he'd never be able to run for anything ever again. In retrospect, the threat probably landed harder than I realized because Anthony was already starting to self-destruct. (It wasn't like what he got caught doing on Twitter didn't exist in other, pre-Twitter formats before then.)

    We started exactly where anyone would when it comes to Anthony Weiner: sex. In his time as a member of the House, Anthony had passed all of one bill. And that one illustrious piece of legislation was to give more visas to models. Yep, protecting the rights of hot women was Anthony's sole achievement in office. That was a good point to make but not an exposé in and of itself. But then our research team noticed something: Anthony had also received campaign contributions from many of the models who received highly coveted H1B visas. Not only was this pay-to-play (give contributions, get government favors), it was illegal. Only American citizens can donate to American political campaigns. He took money from foreign nationals. We gave the story to the *New York Post* and they ran with it. "Weiner's 'Naughty' Hottie$" ran the next day. Because it captured so many of Anthony's flaws in one piece—his lack of actual work, his shallowness, his shady ethics, and of course, his shallow obsession with models—the press ran with it. It wasn't enough to knock Anthony out of the race but it certainly got his attention.

The next one really pissed him off. Anthony played hockey every Tuesday night at Chelsea Piers. He was very proud of it: He thought it made him look athletic and tough. He also never missed a game. Hockey is not that big of a sport in New York and there isn't a lot of space for ice rinks, so getting rink time anywhere is tough. And once you get a regular slot—even if it's at 9 p.m. on Tuesdays—you make sure you're there no matter what. So we knew Anthony was a regular. But many of us had worked in Congress so we also knew that the vote schedule in the House was unpredictable. Endless motions are called on various bills going nowhere, and sometimes those motions come up for a vote at weird hours. Like a Tuesday night at 9 p.m. Sooner or later, Anthony was going to be at Chelsea Piers playing hockey and his colleagues would be voting on legislation critical to our nation's future.

So every Tuesday night, we sent a photographer to Chelsea Piers to gather evidence that Anthony was there. And every Tuesday night, we closely monitored the vote schedule in the House. This went on for weeks. Finally, the stars aligned. He was manning the goal on 23rd Street. His colleagues were casting votes in our nation's capital. And we captured it all. The headline in the *Post* the next day: "Weiner's a Pucking Goof-Off." It drove him batshit crazy. He started complaining to anyone who'd listen about how unfair and rough we were, which was exactly the point. It was starting to register that if he did choose to run, there was a chance he could win, but there was an equally good chance he'd emerge in pieces, his career destroyed, and his reputation shattered. (Of course, he managed to do all of this to himself anyway.)

- **Field:** Voters typically don't pay attention to any election other than a presidential race until about two months before Election Day. (Labor Day is the usual yardstick.) Knocking on voters' doors to encourage them to vote for your candidate probably doesn't do a lot of good if you start too early. So for any campaign with less money and less at stake, canvassing wouldn't begin till the summer. But we needed to appear invincible and omnipresent. So we started canvassing two key areas in early April: Anthony's neighborhood and Anthony's parents' neighborhood. Every night, our volunteers and paid canvassers would start knocking on doors near Weiner-related homes, urging whoever answered to vote for Bloomberg. Of course the door knock itself meant almost nothing that early in the campaign. But when Anthony's mom opened the door and there we were, it sent a message. When Anthony's neighbors all said they'd already been door knocked, it sent a message. When Anthony's childhood neighbors all said they'd already been door knocked, it sent a message.

- **Digital:** Today, banner ads are the least effective form of digital advertising, but in 2009, they were a mainstay. Campaign advertising online was still a relatively new concept, but luckily our digital consultant—Jonah Seiger—understood politics as well as he understood technology, so whatever new idea could be tested out was already on Jonah's to-do list. One day Jonah came to me and said, "You know about geo-targeting, right?" I had no idea what geo-targeting meant. Turns out, it means you can pick a zip code and focus your advertising in just that one area. You can geo-target a small buy. Or you can geo-target a big buy. We decided to geo-target an extremely big buy—in just one zip code: Anthony Weiner's neighborhood. Every time Anthony opened his computer, we wanted him to see us. Every time he logged off, we wanted to be the last thing he saw. So we bought essentially all of the banner ads in Anthony's zip code with the implicit message: If you run, this is going to happen everywhere and it's not going to just say "Bloomberg for Mayor." We already had "Weiner's Naughty Hottie$" and "Weiner's a Pucking Goof-Off" to work with. And it was still early.

• **Lobbying:** Anyone who had any influence with Anthony at all became our obsession. We had lists and lists of connections to Weiner and worked them obsessively to get each of them to call Anthony to tell him that if he ran, they wouldn't support him. Democratic party bosses. Democratic elected officials (especially his colleagues in the House, none of whom wanted to see him become mayor). Union leaders. Donors. Civic leaders. Every day, we went through the list, person by person, and every day, we were able to confirm he'd received yet another call telling him not to run. The calls pissed him off, but he knew he'd need support and money to take on Mike Bloomberg, and the calls made it clear he'd lack both.

• **Paid media:** It was too early to run negative ads on TV against Anthony, especially since he wasn't even a candidate yet. But we knew from our own polling that Mike was up by around fifteen points over Anthony and that we needed to boost the margin to ensure Anthony didn't run. So even though no one is paying attention to the mayoral race in April, we went on the air anyway. Our goal wasn't to influence voters to pick Mike that November.

It was to get them to tell Anthony's pollster that they were for Mike. If you run enough positive ads without anyone on the air against you, you can move your numbers. The support may be soft, but at least short-term, it registers. When our polling came back a few days before Anthony's deadline, we were up seventeen.*

Memorial Day was approaching fast. We had no idea what Anthony was going to do. Some people told us he was running no matter what and everything we did to try to scare him out of the race only made him that much more determined. Others said he knew it was too risky. My gut told me he wouldn't run but I knew our success depended on me being constantly paranoid and constantly finding ten more things we could do rather than just feeling serene and telling everyone not to worry.

Our reverse-engineered polling told us we were in the right place, but whether Anthony's methodology was the same as ours, whether his sample was the same, whether it rained on one of the days he polled and more people were inside, cranky, and told the pollster they were unhappy with Bloomberg was all unknowable.

It was a Monday night. I was at a bar on 13th Street with Scott Stringer, then the Manhattan borough president, trying to convince him to endorse Mike. (It was in vain—he was never going to cross

---

* One thing the press—and I guess Anthony's own team—never realized is that while Mike was always up by around fifteen in every public poll, the margin was always something like 50–33. Reporters would look at it and say "Bloomberg's up by seventeen. He's miles ahead." In reality, this was a huge problem. We couldn't get past 50 percent in our own polling, regardless of how many ads we ran or how many doors we knocked on. And after eight years in office and more than $150 million spent in the first two campaigns alone, the undecideds weren't really undecided. If you weren't for us at that point, you were never going to be. If the press could have accurately read the polling, Weiner might have run, and even if he didn't, we still were vulnerable. That's why the only number that matters in a poll in reelection is "Do you want to reelect x?" How much they're up over an unknown challenger is almost irrelevant.

party lines but I liked Scott and he liked the wooing.) His phone buzzed. So did mine. One nice thing about a drink between two political junkies is that there is no etiquette. You can look at your phone anytime you want. We both did. Scott looked at me and said it before I could: "He's not running."*

---

* Just imagine what would have happened if Anthony did run and he won: All of his sex scandals most likely still would have happened—but at city hall. As a backbench congressman, other than the prurient interest, his downfall had no actual impact on government. If it all happened while he was mayor? Debacle wouldn't begin to capture how bad it would have been. Obviously, it's not like we knew that's what we were saving New York from at the time, but thank god we did.

12

In Politics, Perception Is Reality

You can't feed the media beast without a steady supply of reporter food. One of the challenges of a long-running campaign covered by a relatively small number of reporters is you have to keep them constantly engaged and entertained so they don't start stirring up trouble. The problem is, it's easy to run out of shiny objects. And in our case, distraction was essential since our real goal was far less about persuading voters (at this point, you either liked Mike or you didn't) and far more about making sure no one realized how vulnerable we were.

The first order of business was taking all of the people who could hurt us off the playing field. Some of them—traditional Democratic politicians like Chuck or Kirsten Gillibrand or Andrew Cuomo— would have to endorse the Democratic mayoral nominee but limiting it to one minor press event and nothing else would be a victory. Some of them—major unions like SEIU 1199 (hospital workers), the United Federation of Teachers, 32BJ (janitors and security guards), and the Hotel Trades (hotel workers)—could actually support us, and in other cases, neutrality was also fine. (We didn't accept campaign donations anyway, so we mainly needed them to not help the other guy.) Some of them—traditional Democratic donors—would require a lot of hand holding and we hired what may have been the first-ever campaign antifund-raiser: We didn't want Dara Freed to raise money for Mike— we just wanted her to convince all the major Democratic donors to stay out of the race.

So we were back to the 8 a.m. morning meetings to go through the lists, just like we had with Anthony. To me, we had to infuse the subconscious of every reporter and every insider that Mike's victory was so inevitable that predicting—or trying to bring about—anything else would only make them look foolish. This was a campaign where perception not only had to shape reality, it had to control it. That started with a plan that produced some derision but ultimately succeeded, especially with the reporters mocking us for it.

It seemed a little crazy at the time: an endorsement every single day, seven days a week, from the day we launched the campaign in late March through Election Day. It didn't matter who the endorser was: Sometimes it meant global figures like Al Gore, Colin Powell, or Bono, and sometimes it was hyperlocal organizations like the Korean Grocers Association. What mattered was that it never, ever stopped—that every single day, the big, bad, overwhelmingly powerful Bloomberg campaign machine was sweeping up support from every corner of the city. Most important was the way we announced it: In the press release touting the endorsement, we listed every other person who had already endorsed Mike. (We also filmed a video with every endorser and put it out ourselves to create content and further drive the impression of invincibility.)*

By election day, the list was ten pages long—single-spaced. Most of the endorsements weren't covered and we didn't expect them to be. We just needed the reporters and insiders to glance at the announcement, glance at the growing list of supporters, and say to themselves, somewhere in the deep recesses of their brains, *Shit, these guys have everyone locked up.* Because once they thought that, believing that Thompson had a chance was silly.† And if no one believed Thompson had a chance, no one had a reason to spend any real time, money, or political capital helping him.

We probably did go overboard on endorsements once. I was obsessed with trying to increase support and turnout from small ethnic communities around the city that were typically ignored by campaigns and could provide a handful of votes here and there to help get us over the top. That meant radio ads and print ads in Thai, Korean, Hindi, Russian, Bengali, and Vietnamese, in addition to the usual spots in English, Spanish, and Mandarin (along with a few in Cantonese). It meant courting leaders of every ethnic community—no matter how little known—if we thought they had influence over local voters. And in one case, it meant securing the endorsement of a high-profile Bollywood star.

Shilpa Shetty was one of the biggest Bollywood stars in the world. And she was coming to New York to serve as the honorary grand

---

* I never would have learned how to work this intensely or quickly if I hadn't worked for Chuck. Speed is an underrated skill and Chuck grooms it in all of his people.

† Gaming out the focus of reporters was a constant process. At one point, we realized that most newsrooms have NY1 on all day, playing silently in the background and nothing else. So if we ran positive campaign ads on NY1 and negative campaign ads bashing our opponent everywhere else, odds were that reporters would only see the positive ads and not write about the attacks (while every shred of evidence shows that negative ads work, reporters and voters still have to pretend they don't like it), which is exactly what we did.

marshal of the Indian Day Parade. I decided we should get her to endorse Mike at the parade and we could then broadcast that widely to the Indian community. We didn't know her, but we were able to get to her manager through a tangled web of connections. We were told she loved Mike Bloomberg (which seemed doubtful, but, whatever) and was happy to do it. Great.

The night before the parade, we got a call from her manager asking when they should expect payment. What are you talking about? we asked. For the endorsement, naturally. We explained that in the United States, people don't pay for political endorsements. Why would she do it? he asked. He wasn't wrong, but we also obviously weren't going to give them any money. So much for Shilpa Shetty.

But then the day of the parade came. Mike was marching, which meant our videographer would be there anyway. And because he was with Mike, he had access to the entire parade route. This is a long shot, I told him, but just go up to her and ask her what she thinks of Mike Bloomberg. Maybe she'll say something we can use.

Turns out she was aware of our refusal to pay and wasn't happy about it. But when our videographer asked her for the eighth time what she thought of Mike Bloomberg, she finally replied, "Fine, fine already. I like him. He's a great mayor." We had our endorsement.

"Go. Go. Run back to the office," I told Barnett Zitron, our videographer.

"But the parade isn't over yet."

"Just go. Before she realizes what we did."

We ran back to the office, edited her sound bite into a clip and posted it on YouTube. We then took out ads in the Indian weekly papers touting our support from Bollywood's Shilpa Shetty. I don't know if any Indian voters actually cared. Maybe a few did. And I don't know if Shilpa Shetty or her people even noticed. But when the press corps covering the mayoral race saw this one, you knew they shook their heads and just said, "These fucking guys are everywhere."

We repeated the same approach internally too. Good campaigns don't happen by accident—they're run by smart, hardworking people. The more talent the other side had, the more of a threat they posed. And since we had a mayor who was popular among many Democrats and since we had an unlimited budget, we thought, why not take everyone off the table? Kevin Sheekey—Mike's longtime iconoclastic political Svengali—asked me to meet with Howard Wolfson about him joining the campaign.

Howard rose to fame as Hillary Clinton's communications chief but had worked in the trenches of Democratic politics for years. From Chuck's first Senate race to running the Democratic Congressional Campaign Committee's press, Howard is probably the nation's foremost mind when it comes to political communications. In late 2008, he'd also just come off the disastrous Hillary Clinton presidential campaign—a campaign marred by constant infighting between multiple factions. Howard took some of the public blame for the campaign's dysfunction, so when Kevin asked me to meet with him, I was a little skeptical. Why would I want to bring the toxicity of Hillary's campaign to ours?

But since Kevin both outranked me in Bloomberg world and was (and still is) an extremely smart guy, I met with Howard anyway. I didn't need to ask about his abilities or qualifications. They were evident. Instead, I asked why I shouldn't worry about the same thing happening to us that happened to Hillary. His answer was so succinct—"I can't afford to have that happen in another campaign"—and so on point, it personified everything I soon came to love about him. He didn't try to point fingers at Mark Penn, his chief antagonist. He didn't try to bullshit me with the great lessons he'd learned and how he'd grown as a person. He just gave me an honest, intelligent, thoughtful, and irrefutable answer.*

Howard understood something both intellectually and intuitively that most people in politics and communications just don't get. The best spin is no spin. Rather than triaging and obfuscating and boasting and attacking, just answer the question honestly, thoughtfully, and simply. Reporters have built-in bullshit detectors. The more you try to spin them, the more you just convince them that there's something more to the story than you're telling them. You're just digging your own grave. Whatever it is, own it. Explain why you did whatever you did. Why you decided whatever you decided. Assuming you were logical in how you went about whatever it was, whether you got it right or wrong, people can at least understand what happened and that's all most reporters want: for things to make sense.† You can always tell a

---

* Howard did this again in my defense to great effect. Wayne Barrett, a legendary reporter for the *Village Voice*, decided that I was the devil incarnate and he would be the one to expose it. This was toward the end of Wayne's career and he wasn't totally with it anymore, so the piece blamed me for Blagojevich, for Lehman's collapse, for the destruction of the global economy, and I think he may have fingered me for Jimmy Hoffa's disappearance. The *Voice* wasn't important anymore but a muckraking piece by Wayne still had the potential to ripple through the media. Howard's defense of me was genius. Rather than arguing a single point in the story or attacking Wayne's credibility or even his mental stability, he just said, "Wayne Barrett is the best investigative reporter in America. He spent six thousand words on Bradley and didn't find a single thing. That's the best vindication anyone could ever want." He flipped it on Wayne—using the craziness of Wayne's piece to establish Wayne had nothing on me—by leveraging Wayne's own credibility. It was brilliant. And not a single reporter followed up on Wayne's story—it was almost as if it had never run.

† This lesson proved useful in 2017 when I closed up shop on our failing effort to replace Bill de Blasio as mayor of New York City. Our entire effort was predicated on de Blasio being vulnerable because of the multiple criminal investigations into his administration and campaign. When the U.S. attorney and the district attorney both announced that while they believed de Blasio had behaved unethically and illegally, there wasn't enough evidence to bring charges, it was clear that we wouldn't be able to recruit anyone into the race capable of unseating the incumbent. We put out a statement that morning thanking the prosecutors for doing a thorough review and announcing that without indictments, there was no path to beating de Blasio. On calls with reporters that day, I said simply that the strategy was based on indictments, there were no indictments, and so there was no path to victory. By owning it, everyone accepted my explanation, I received a minimal amount of grief and snark (even on Twitter, except from the usual congenital assholes), and they moved on.

more sophisticated comms professional from an amateur based on how much they try to use spin and bluster. The good ones never need to.

We then brought in a series of high-profile local Democrats, including Maura Keaney to run field, Karen Keogh to help secure endorsements, and Dara Freed to convince donors to not give to Thompson. They all got some grief from hard-core Dems over it (especially Howard) but instead of spending all of our time trying to counter people like Howard, Maura, Karen, and Dara, we forced the other side to try to counter them.*

We repeated the same process on every front: getting unions in our corner, getting local elected officials in our corner, demonstrating inevitability by advertising heavily from the day we went up to skew the Weiner numbers through Election Day (spending $109 million in total, most of it on TV), knocking on more than two million doors throughout the campaign, and so on. Omnipresent and hyperactive meant ensuring the narrative remained that the race was out of reach for Thompson. For as long as Democratic insiders believed that, the race remained Bloomberg versus Bloomberg.

But there was one very big wild card. I didn't take Barack Obama's class in law school. He was this new guy. There were all these legal superstars and Nobel Prize winners on the faculty. Why waste time with him? Shows what I know. I didn't get to know Obama until I became deputy governor and the first thing he said to me when we met in Springfield was, "You didn't take my class." It was hard not to like him.

Mike had stayed out of the 2008 presidential race. He thought about running. He was a finalist to be VP for McCain.† McCain had

---

* They couldn't. Thompson's communications shop was terrified of Howard especially.

† Although possibly without Mike's consent. Mike kept telling Kevin he didn't want to be vice president and Kevin kept sending in the vetting to the McCain campaign anyway. Mike probably

supported Mike aggressively in 2001 when virtually no one else did. But Mike also knew Obama would win and as mayor, he needed to do what was best for New York City, so he stayed out of the race. That meant Obama owed us nothing and in any normal world, the incredibly popular, dynamic new president would swoop into New York City, raise some money, hold an event endorsing the Democratic candidate for mayor, maybe even cut an ad for the Democrat, and go back to D.C. Given our margin for error, the last thing we could afford was Obama putting his weight behind Thompson. No one was excited about Thompson. You either liked Mike and were with us or you didn't and you were against us. Thompson being a nonfactor was a critical part of our strategy.

So now we had a new subcampaign to obsess over: Operation Keep Obama Neutral.* We drew a map of every connection we had to Obama, and then armed each of them with the same message: "Mike stayed out of your race, he's your best conduit to Wall Street and best pro-business validator for many of your policies, so stay out of his." Every day, I'd check the map, see where we had openings, where each person on our list had last talked to the targets on their list, and push, push, and push some more. For example:

- Geoffrey Canada, the founder of Harlem Children's Zone—one of the first great charter schools in America—knew Valerie Jarrett. She trusted his opinion and Geoff and Mike were close. Geoff worked Valerie for us.

---

meant it but when the potential next president of the United States asks you to be his running mate, it's hard to say no.

* For anyone reading this book who's thinking of working in tech or politics, hopefully this all makes it clear that if you are not extremely neurotic and paranoid—if you aren't constantly inventing a new reason to worry about something—this is not the business for you.

- Patti Harris developed a relationship with not only Valerie Jarrett but also Susan Axelrod, David Axelrod's wife. Susan founded and runs CURE, a foundation dedicated to fighting epilepsy, and knew it made sense to know Mike's closest—and brilliant—adviser. Patti has far more power, influence, and strategic direction in Bloomberg world than anyone (other than Mike himself).

- Mike developed a relationship with Rahm Emanuel (who had become Obama's chief of staff). Rahm saw Mike as a kindred spirit and more important, a useful ally and surrogate for the White House. Rahm's agenda wasn't impacted by Bill Thompson or whoever served as mayor of New York City. But Mike's credibility as a business leader could be useful to Obama.

- Kevin went to John Podesta. Podesta ran Obama's transition (and later served as chief of staff). Podesta's think tank—the Center for American Progress—had common views with Mike on issues like immigration, and we sought his endorsement. In an event next to the Eleanor Roosevelt statue in Riverside Park, Podesta, Planned Parenthood President Cecile Richards, and former SEIU President Dennis Rivera all endorsed Mike. That meant something.

- ObamaCare. It was impossible to get Mike to take a position he didn't support, but fortunately, he supported the Affordable Care Act. And in Mike's world, support doesn't just mean saying so during a press conference about trash pickup. It meant getting the word out and lending his resources. That meant a phone blitz to three hundred thousand constituents making the case for the bill and for signing up on the local exchange. Whether or not it was appreciated by the White House, the ease by which we could reach so many people so quickly must have been noted.

———————————————

It was now October. We'd managed to neutralize everyone else who mattered: SEIU and the UFT both declared neutrality; 32BJ, the Hotel Trades, the Building Trades, and four dozen other unions had endorsed us; we'd secured the endorsement of every weekly and ethnic paper in the city but one; and knew support from the *Times, Post,* and *Daily News* was on the way. We'd lined up all of the city's major clergy, we'd met our goal of an endorsement every single day, we'd knocked Weiner out of the race, and we'd kept Thompson from raising any real money. We were doing everything we could to generate excitement for Mike but our millions of door knocks and tens of millions of dollars spent on ads weren't moving the needle much. We just had to make it to Election Day without any major hiccup and we'd probably squeak through. A vigorous endorsement from Obama for Thompson qualified as a major hiccup.

We got a call from the White House. The president was coming to New York. He was going to stop by an event that Thompson would also be at, issue a very nominal endorsement of the Democratic candidate but not give a speech, not talk to reporters, not take photos with him, not appear at a campaign rally, not film an ad, not record a robo call—nothing but a very perfunctory Friday-afternoon endorsement.

We could live with it. I would have preferred nothing at all, but considering this was the Democratic nominee for the mayor of the most important city in the country and the newly elected Democratic president, both of whom were African American, a nonendorsement

endorsement was acceptable. (And, of course, we took every nice thing Obama ever said about Mike—and Obama had made sure to say plenty—and plastered them in ads so to the casual observer, if Obama had endorsed anyone, it was us.)

Election Day finally came. In some ways, it was a relief to see all of our plans fulfilled. In other ways, the true test of whether we were right and whether we pulled it off was up to the voters. Our final poll showed us right at 50 percent, with Thompson at 45 percent and the rest undecided or for minor party candidates. At best, the polling would hold, we'd win by a few points, but we'd also see our three-card-monte strategy exposed to the world. At worst, despite all of our strategy, all of our work, all the money, we'd still come up short.

Election Day is always frustrating because there's not that much left to do. We had get-out-the-vote efforts all over the city. Millions of robo calls, all finely micro-targeted so the right voter would receive a message from the right messenger, were sent throughout the day and night. Final ads were on the air. Turnout was low, but that wasn't necessarily bad. One of the risks of our strategy was that our own supporters would think we were inevitable and not bother to vote.* I knew we'd win but I also knew what it'd mean for me if we lost: first Rod, then Lehman, then managing to somehow lose Mike's reelection campaign. Sure, I was generally seen as the one honest, competent guy in the Blagojevich inner circle. And I had as much to do with Lehman's collapse as you did. But as our entire thesis for the campaign proved, sometimes, optics are everything.

We headed over to the Sheraton for the election-night festivities.

---

* This was even a problem within the campaign where much of our own staff were buying the same hype as everyone else. If we can't lose, why work all night? Why work on weekends? I imposed an "everyone works till 8 p.m." edict that some people on the team appreciated, but many did not. Howard even had to kill a Page Six item about complaints from anonymous members of the team that I was forcing them to work too hard.

We rented a suite for the senior team to receive the results from each precinct and figure out where we were. At first, things looked great. NBC News wanted to call the race for Mike the minute the polls closed. But they were still working off of our narrative rather than actual election results. And the reality was, the race was close, as we knew and feared it would be since the day we overturned term limits. The numbers started coming in. They were pretty evenly split, which you'd expect when the losing candidate wasn't going to do worse than 45 percent. Then, by 10 p.m., some of the Democratic strongholds came in—Central Brooklyn, Southeast Queens—and we were suddenly losing. I knew rationally that once the more moderate precincts reported, we'd be back on top. But that thinking was dictated by logic, by data, by assumptions. What if those assumptions were wrong?

Now it was 10:30 p.m. The polls had been closed for an hour and a half. We were still down. I saw Maura and her team on the phone, writing down numbers. I saw a few smiles creep onto their faces. Our votes were coming in. Soon, we were ahead—not by much, but ahead. And we stayed ahead. The final tally was 50.7 percent for Mike, 46.3 percent for Thompson, and the rest for minor candidates.

The rest of the night and the next day were a little embarrassing. I had been hoping to somehow defy the numbers and win by a healthy margin anyway. And since the results played out exactly as we expected, it meant everyone realized what we had just spent the past year doing. (In anticipation of this, we sat down with Michael Barbaro of the *Times* right before Election Day to take him through all of our thinking, strategy, and execution; we embargoed the story till after the polls closed.)

I knew I was about to start my own consulting firm. I knew the business—at least in the first year or two—would be based almost entirely on my reputation, and I wasn't sure what running a campaign based on distraction would mean for my reputation. I also didn't know the first thing about running a business. Then again, I didn't know how to be a deputy governor or run a mayoral campaign. Those worked out. How hard could it be?

SECTION III

Creating the Language of Tech and Politics

13

If You're Really Ambitious, Create Your Own Market

$234,000. It was a lot more money than I'd ever had. And it was the amount left over after taxes from the bonus Mike gave me for winning the election. It was also our entire savings, so however long it lasted was how long I could give my own business a try. Once I was down to about $50,000, it'd be time to go find a job.

Howard and I had started talking about creating a consulting firm together earlier in the summer, and we recruited Gary Ginsberg, a corporate PR expert, to join us. We figured between our respective skills and credentials (Gary ran communications for Rupert Murdoch at NewsCorp), people would hire us. But then Mike pressed Howard to join the administration as a deputy mayor and Gary got a lucrative offer to run PR at Time Warner, so by Thanksgiving, it was just me. We were still wrapping up the campaign so I had a little time to figure things out. I knew I didn't want to go back into government. I knew from my days at Lehman that I didn't like working for a big company.

And I liked the idea of being entrepreneurial and creating something new.

I had never been that focused on making money, but in the back of my head, I figured that eventually, when the time was right, I'd come up with a way to take all of my skills, experiences, and relationships and turn them into a business. The time was right. But without Howard and Gary, both of whom were older, well known, and better connected in the corporate world, just trying the exact same approach of hanging out a shingle, calling everyone I knew, and assuming business would come in didn't make sense. I needed something different, something that took advantage of my skills and put them to use in a way no one else could really do.

Most people in political consulting have a specific skill they sell: lobbying, PR, polling, making ads, opposition research, and so on. Or, if they run campaigns, they focus on a specific jurisdiction like Washington, D.C., or a particular state capital. I was good at taking a hard problem, figuring out how to solve it, and then making sure everything was executed through to completion. And between my work in New York City, Washington, Illinois, and traversing the country from state capital to state capital during my time at Lehman, I didn't need to focus on just one jurisdiction.

The most interesting type of role to me was running big, complex multijurisdictional campaigns for people with a lot of money and a lot at stake. I'd be the campaign manager for, say, Walmart, when they had to get zoning approvals to open stores in ten big cities, or for Expedia, when they had to fight off proposed taxes on online travel booking in twelve states. I'd figure out the strategy, build a team in each market, and run it like a campaign. I couldn't point to any businesses that had that model but that didn't mean we couldn't be the first—especially if we worked harder than everyone else.

During the mayoral race, I'd send Mike an email at 5 a.m. every day saying who that day's endorsement was from and everything going on in the campaign that day: field, ads, polling, events, etc. Since Mike didn't really like politics, he was happy to get my email, find out what he needed to know, and then go on with his day being mayor. Getting something that organized, that early in the morning also didn't hurt his opinion of me: I came off as hardworking, organized, persistent, and thoughtful.

Why not do the same thing at Tusk Strategies? We'd send our clients an email every morning at 7 a.m. listing what was happening in their campaign that day: every market, every issue, every tactic. Clients would wake up and see what was going on. The contrast between our proactivity and most consultants only doing what they're asked after being asked a few times would be a benefit, plus it'd keep me and the client on the same page; we'd have an agenda for the day and it'd make it easier to get things done.*

So Tusk Strategies would be a campaign management firm that handled big campaigns all over the country. Since this type of firm didn't exist, I figured I could set the market for our work. I thought about the biggest fee I could ask for with a straight face, settled on $25,000 a month, and decided that was the floor—if someone wasn't willing to pay that, we weren't willing to work for them.

Of course, since no one was aware that we existed—or even that the type of service we were offering existed—our competition was really ourselves. We had to convince people that whatever they needed done was so important that spending an extra $25,000 a month—on

---

* We've done this every day since January 2, 2010. The emails no longer come from me but every client and every portfolio company gets a daily update at 7 a.m. This accomplishes three things: (1) the clients love it, (2) it keeps everyone focused and in sync, and (3) it's a great management tool because if my employees have to report to me and to the client every single day and they're not actually doing the work and constantly coming up with new ideas, it becomes painfully obvious very quickly.

top of paying the lobbyists, PR firms, pollsters, and everyone else—was worth it. It meant we wouldn't ever have a lot of clients at once, and it meant in most cases, the only people with the budget and authority to add us to the team was someone from the C-suite, frequently the CEO.

It was a great business model in that I'd found a niche no one else had, and as long as at least some clients were willing to pay the fee, I could create the market. It was also an awful business model in that it couldn't ever scale that much, it was labor intensive, and if we ended up with more clients than I could handle myself, I'd have to bring in people with similar abilities and backgrounds and pay them a lot. But either way, it was mine. It was my model, based on my experiences, my skills, and my interests. If it succeeded, it was a reflection of everything I'd done, of who I was. If it failed, it'd also be a reflection of me, but at least I'd have failed on my own accord.

We didn't start with much. Shelley Capito, my assistant from the campaign, was brave enough to join me and become our first employee. My friends from Parks—Stuart Ruderfer and David Cohn—had started a successful marketing firm and gave us desks in their office. We started off with one client—Camelot, the operator of the UK Lottery—whom I knew from my Lehman days. I was running around, trying to gin up business, trying to land clients, trying to get the word out about our work.

I ran into some trouble early on when I started helping Harold Ford Jr.—a former congressman from Memphis—explore a Senate run in New York. (When Hillary Clinton became secretary of state, her Senate seat opened up and then–New York Governor David Patterson appointed Kirsten Gillibrand to fill the seat; at the time, Gillibrand was not well known and the seat was up just a year later so she was potentially vulnerable to a challenger.) Harold, as it turns out, had zero intention of actually running. He just wanted to get attention from the press (what do you expect—he's a politician) and promote his upcoming book. That meant attacking the status quo to make his candidacy seem more realistic, and in one case, he attacked Chuck (who was a strong supporter of Gillibrand's and felt like no one should primary her without his permission). I told Harold to leave Chuck alone and that I wouldn't keep helping him if he kept going after Chuck—and he stopped. But there's nothing worse for Chuck than a bad story, he blamed it on me, and we never reconciled.*

Harold didn't run, and while Camelot's fee was enough to avoid having to raid the bonus Mike gave me, one client wasn't my definition of success. Then the phone rang. Kevin Sheekey. "Are you free for breakfast tomorrow with me, Joel Klein, Paul Tudor Jones, Stan Druckenmiller, and Ken Langone?" Was I free to meet with three billionaires, the NYC schools chancellor, and a deputy mayor? Yes. Yes I was.

What did all of these people have in common? Charter schools. Mike was a big proponent of charter schools and one of Joel's main accomplishments as chancellor (there were many) was to build a strong network of charter schools in New York City. Paul, Stan, and Ken were all major donors to local charter schools. But there was a problem (which was music to my ears—no one hires us unless there's a problem). New York State law limited the number of charter schools that could be authorized in New York City. They were at the limit. Mike, Joel, and Kevin tried to pass legislation in Albany to lift the cap, but they lost. They needed a real campaign. And Paul, Ken, and Stan were willing to raise and donate the money for it.

On the merits, the fight made sense. While ed reformers love to

---

* This experience was enough for me to realize it didn't make sense to advise political candidates. By definition, almost anyone running for office wants the validation that comes with it more than anything. If they think you're the brain that can get them there, they want to talk to you all day, every day, about everything—their hopes, their dreams, their fears. It's too much. You can't run a business like that.

frame charters as the panacea for all of our country's education woes and while teachers' unions love to frame charters as the root of all evil, the reality is that neither is true. Some charter schools are highly effective and do a much better job educating kids than the local public schools do in the same neighborhood. Others are poorly run, ineffective, and should be shut down. But the good ones—Success Academy, KIPP, Achievement First—show that when you can remove the albatross of the rules and procedures governing how schools are typically run and replace that with a far more logical approach, you can do a lot better. If they're able to reward good teachers, remove bad teachers, avoid a lot of unnecessary bureaucracy that comes with being part of a big public school system, raise philanthropic money, and put much tougher expectations and standards on students, then parents, teachers, and administrators can work miracles in the right hands. Making it possible for more of those miracles to occur made sense to me.

So of course I wanted the opportunity. But Albany was controlled by the teachers' unions. And the teachers' unions hated charter schools because charter school teachers aren't unionized. Did I really want to take their money and put my reputation on the line for a campaign we probably couldn't win?

At the end of the breakfast, I proposed, "Let's do some polling. We know the powers that be in Albany will start out against this. But if we have compelling arguments with overwhelming public support, maybe we can sway them."

Barack Obama and Arne Duncan gave us those arguments. In 2009, the Obama administration created a program called Race to the Top. They took a relatively small amount of federal money—$8 billion—and made it available to any state that could implement a host of education reforms. The most innovative states would win grants worth hundreds of millions of dollars. Eight billion dollars is a pittance compared to the amount of money spent on schools across the country every year. If it were just handed out to the states, half of them wouldn't even notice. But once it became a competition, everything changed. By definition, politics is a competitive business, filled with competitive people, and once it became about winning and losing, every politician wanted to win. (This is exactly what Obama and Duncan were counting on.) All of a sudden, states were passing major reforms to their laws around helping charter schools, assessing teachers based on performance, and making it easier to remove bad teachers from the classroom.

New Yorkers weren't interested enough in Albany politics to rise up against the teachers' unions and force their state reps and state senators to authorize more charter schools. But New Yorkers were fed up with high taxes and fees. They were fed up with the low quality of many public schools. They were fed up with Albany's endemic corruption. And so a campaign based around winning Race to the Top—which required lifting the charter cap—could appeal to them.

When we asked people whether they felt their legislators should do whatever it takes to win Race to the Top and secure $700 million in new federal funding for our schools, 92 percent said yes—and over 70 percent felt strongly about it. Those are remarkable numbers. New Yorkers love to complain about anything. Ninety-two percent of New Yorkers wouldn't necessarily agree that the Second Coming on the Great Lawn in Central Park would be a good thing. But they overwhelmingly supported winning Race to the Top.

That was our hook. I put together a campaign strategy, presented it to the group, and Ken hosted a fund-raiser to raise the money for the campaign. I estimated we'd need $8 million to run TV ads, radio ads, conduct grassroots outreach, and more. Neil Newhouse, our pollster, walked everyone through what he found. I explained how we could use that to put Democratic legislators who normally automatically side with the teachers unions in a bind and force them to move forward on new charters.

Other than the elevator on the way down from Ken's home suddenly stopping, bouncing off the corridor walls, us hearing a snapping sound and realizing that if we plummeted to our death, the headline would be, "Four billionaires, charter school visionary Geoffrey Canada, and a few other guys die in freak elevator accident"* (the fire department hacked through the elevator door with an ax, and we jumped down into someone's apartment, surprising and confusing them as a parade of people they recognized walked through their kitchen to the back stairwell), things went well.

One upside of being an upstart is the entrenched interests never see you coming. I lived that lesson with Uber—the taxi owners reacted way too late to stop us. I live it every day with all of the startups in our portfolio and the established companies we're disrupting. But I learned the lesson thanks to our charter school fight.

All of our media—TV ads, radio ads, print ads, digital ads—centered around the message of "don't let Albany blow $700 million of your money," putting the blame squarely on the state legislature if New York failed to win Race to the Top. We put up posters all over New York City and Albany saying, "Missing: $700 Million" with a background of stacks of cash and an explanation of the issue.

It all helped produce an unlikely ally in John Sampson. Sampson is now in prison for corruption, but at the time, he was the majority leader of the New York State Senate. Everyone assumed he'd just follow the party line and do what the teachers' unions told him. Sampson clearly has many flaws but he saw what charter schools meant to his

---

* The "other guys" were me, Joe Williams—the founder of Democrats for Education Reform and a legendary ed reform warrior—and John Petry, a hedge fund manager who probably will be a billionaire one day and is an incredibly committed ed reform advocate.

community. He and his caucus gave us about twenty votes and, combined with Republican support, we shocked everyone by passing our charter expansion bill through the senate and into the assembly.

Sheldon Silver, the former speaker of the assembly (also indicted for corruption), was the single biggest beneficiary of teachers' unions campaign largess and had no intention of passing our bill. But he assumed it'd never even get to him. Suddenly, it passed through a Democratic-led senate. We were blitzing the airwaves. We had charter parents visiting the district offices of every state rep. We kept up an incessant pace of calls from constituents to their state reps, making it seem like this was the only issue in the world anyone cared about.

We then started getting public support for expanding charter schools from leading Democrats: Arne Duncan, Bill Clinton, Al Sharpton, Andrew Cuomo. The pressure became too much to bear. Silver sat down with Mike Bloomberg's legislative team—led by Howard and Micah Lasher, Mike's then-head of legislative affairs in Albany—and cut a deal.

The bill authorized a hundred and twenty-five thousand more charter seats across the state. That meant an *annual* additional state contribution of $2 billion to charters (because the state pays for charter students, just like it does public school students). We agreed not to authorize any new for-profit charters. (Our supporters didn't like the for-profit charters anyway.) The lead story in the next day's *Times* highlighted Mike's huge win. New York then won the entire $700 million in Race to the Top funding. And because this was the first ed reform campaign run like a political campaign, we became the firm to call if you had an education-related problem. (We ended up helping Michelle Rhee create StudentsFirst, helping NBC News create Education Nation, and running ed reform campaigns in cities and states all over the country.)

Now that I've been running a business for eight years, I've learned that clients come and go in waves, often for no good reason. It's kind of like sports—sometimes you're just hot and every plate appearance is a hit and sometimes you're not and nothing new comes in. You're the same person in both situations. You didn't get any smarter or dumber. You didn't work any harder or less hard. It's just random— and everyone I know in any sort of client-services business feels the exact same way.*

All of a sudden, business started flowing in. Walmart wanted to enter New York City and hired us to run the campaign. Expedia wanted grassroots campaigns around the country to fight off attempts by the hotel industry to impose new taxes on online travel booking. Taubman wanted help getting zoning approvals to build a new mall. We started hiring more employees. Got our own office. Another fifteen to twenty years at this pace and I could probably retire.

Then yet another call came in that changed everything. Kevin again. I was sitting in a Walmart meeting in the spring of 2011. I stepped out to take the call.

"Hey. There's this guy with a small transportation startup. He's having some regulatory problems. Would you mind talking to him?"

---

* We looked hard at incubating a startup that would create a marketplace for public-affairs services like lobbying, PR, and polling. Right now, there's no systematic way for sellers to find clients or for buyers to find vendors so it's all ad hoc and often based on recommendations that are more predicated on referral fees than anything else. A marketplace would help everyone on both sides of the transaction by making the entire industry available, transparent, and easily reachable. The problem was making the marketplace profitable. Most marketplaces work by taking a small piece of every transaction. That works for startups like Airbnb where all of the transactions are one-time occasions. In our model, once the customer and vendor got to know each other, there was no way to keep them from just transacting off-platform and cutting us out of the picture.

14

When to Beg for Forgiveness

n the wake of Travis Kalanick's exit from Uber in 2017, hundreds of thousands of words across columns, blogs, articles, and even books have all been dedicated to the reasons for his undoing. While the issues around his tenure at Uber didn't particularly come up in my work with him, that doesn't make them any less credible or valid.* And even in our interactions around government and politics, he (like everyone) had his flaws. But fear of making a decision is not one of them. Some clients take months and months of dillydallying before they hire you.

---

* Having spent far too much time thinking about this, my best sense of what happened at Uber is that it took someone like Travis—driving, competitive, brilliant, visionary, ruthless—to launch the concept and turn it into an actual business. But once the skill set of being CEO evolved from creating something entirely new to managing a $70 billion bureaucracy, Travis's skills were less crucial and his weaknesses more glaring. The appointment of Dara Khosrowshahi reflected a change Uber needed to make to adapt to its new reality (and he has excelled in the role). Uber is both an inspiring tale and a cautionary tale, which is what makes it so interesting.

Travis hired us that day. (I got really lucky when he called back a second time and said, "I can't afford your whole fee. Would you be willing to take part of it in equity?" Given that Uber's valuation grew more than 250 times since then, thank god I said yes.)

At the time, Uber was a brand-new company. They were only operating in San Francisco and had already faced down the California Public Utilities Commission over what types of permits they needed. Now they were in New York, and soon after launching, received a cease and desist letter from the New York City Taxi and Limousine Commission (TLC). A cease and desist letter is never good. It means either you have to stop operating entirely or you have to convince a bureaucracy that they're wrong. For most startups, the first option is unacceptable and the second one isn't much better.

Travis didn't know anyone who knew New York politics. So he called Matt Cohler, a partner at Benchmark and one of Uber's earliest investors. Matt didn't know anyone either but he knew Steve Ratner, who managed Mike Bloomberg's money. Steve called Kevin and Kevin called me.

Travis came to New York a few days later. We were still working out of Stuart and David's office at the time and he spent a few hours in their conference room walking me through what Uber was—their strategy, vision, operations, regulatory perspective, and challenges.

I still vividly remember him saying to me, "One day, Tusk, no one's going to own a car. All cars will drive themselves. And you'll be able to get one just by pressing a button."

For all of the challenges Travis faced over the years, including losing control of his own company, he saw the future before anyone else did *and,* over the next five years, he did more to make that future a reality than anyone else in the world. He took a random German word—Uber—and turned it into not only a household name, but a verb. ("I'll Uber home from the bar.")

At first, I wasn't totally sure what to make of him. He had a ton of energy. A ton of ideas. Like me, he paced when he walked and unlike me, he wrote everything on a whiteboard. He liked to talk through every idea, sometimes for too long, but he worked things out in his head by pacing, writing, and talking until he knew what he wanted to do. In some ways, he was a lot like a new, energizing political candidate: He had a vision, strong beliefs, an intense work ethic, and he wanted everyone to know it, as quickly as possible. Working with Travis was totally different from the corporate clients we'd been working with: far more exciting, much faster paced, more innovative, with higher stakes. It felt a lot like a campaign. We were constantly gaming out the fight with the TLC—what we'd do in response to each possible action and reaction, and who and what firepower we could bring to the fight. At the time, it didn't dawn on me that my own future was going to revolve around the nexus of tech and politics, but it felt right.

A memo I wrote Travis in mid-2011 laying out my initial thoughts on how Uber should deal with its New York City problem ended up encompassing many of the same tactics we'd use over the next five years to fight the taxi industry: In every jurisdiction, make taxi's opposition all about their own corrupt, entrenched needs, and not about the good of drivers or riders; align Uber with any elected official who really cared about technology and innovation; draw attention to taxi's long and ugly history of racism; posit Uber as a way to fundamentally change that; and demonstrate that Uber drivers were all individual small businesses and this was a new and different type of opportunity for them. Taxi's strength was their political influence. We needed to make it their weakness.

We started getting Travis exposure. He met with Mike's digital czar, Rachel Stern, to talk about his vision and what Uber could mean for the city's growing tech sector. We talked to Rob Walsh, the city's Small Business Services commissioner, so he could start thinking about how Uber drivers were each a small business in their own right. And of course, we started talking to TLC chairman David Yassky and his staff to make sure they understood what Uber was—a platform connecting drivers and riders—and wasn't—a taxi service. It took a while to draw the distinction.

On one hand, it seemed obvious: Uber didn't own any cars and didn't employ any drivers. It just connected drivers who wanted customers with people who wanted a ride. On the other hand, what was it then? It was more tangible than say, Sprint or AT&T, where you may use their service to physically call for a car, but the phone company otherwise has nothing to do with the transaction. The TLC took a while to wrap their heads around it (we ended up convincing them by literally signing an affidavit affirming what Uber was and wasn't) but since they worked for tech pioneer Mike Bloomberg who really wanted to diversify the city's economy by growing the tech sector, and since Mike didn't take campaign contributions so the usual influence the taxi industry has over politicians didn't apply, they were able to get there. This, of course, proved to be an entirely different dynamic than what we had to deal with in every other jurisdiction.

One afternoon after meeting with the TLC, we were sitting at the crappy conference table in my office, hypothesizing about next steps.

"You know, Tusk, we can just turn everyone on and flood the TLC with complaints if we need to," Travis said.

"From our customers or our drivers?"

"Both probably, but especially our customers."

"You think they care that much about you to take time out of their day to email some regulator?"

"Look at what they have now. Taxis are dirty. The drivers don't know how to get where you want to go half the time. Even if they have a credit card scanner, they tell you it's broken to try to make you pay in cash. Everything we offer is much better."

Having gotten to know the product, I didn't disagree. But preferring one mode of transportation to another and actually speaking up on a local policy issue are two very different things.

"Okay, fine. Let's say you're right. What makes you think the TLC will even care?"

"You tell me. Don't they answer to the people?"

"No. They answer to the mayor's office. Their world is mainly the taxi medallion owners and the drivers. If they really cared about innovation, the system wouldn't be this bad in the first place."

"Does the mayor's office care?"

I thought about it for a moment. "This one in particular? About innovation, yes. About emails from your customers? No. Mike doesn't really care that much about politics in the first place so he's not going to let a bunch of emails tell him what to do."

I stopped and thought some more. "But in other places, yes. Your average politician is pretty much the opposite of Mike. So if they're really hearing from a lot of voters? Yeah. Definitely. It could matter."

Travis stepped up to the whiteboard and started writing. "Okay. So we have customers who can speak up but it only works in places where you have a politician in charge who just wants to be liked."

"Right. Provided the people speaking up are actually voters."

"Most of our customers are local. Shouldn't be a problem."

"Good. If you think about it, Airbnb couldn't really do this because all the scale happens on the guest side and by definition, the guests aren't from there. So they're not voters there. This wouldn't work for everyone. But it could work for us."

He stopped pacing and went back to the whiteboard. "So we need local voters to speak up, we need enough of them, we need to be in a place where the local politician in charge of our issue just wants to do whatever's popular. What else?"

"If we're talking about entering a market and then turning our riders on the politicians who try to shut us down, it also matters what the politicians can do to us in return."

"The lawyers already looked into this. It's pretty much fines. Towing cars. Stuff like that."

"No jail time? Nothing criminal?"

"Nope."

"So those are just costs of doing business. Fine. To be clear, it'd be different if you were looking at an indictment. I've testified in a few trials. Not fun. At all." I'm not sure Travis would have backed down even then.

He started writing again on the whiteboard. *Cost of doing business. Legal risks.* "What else? What about the press?"

"Good question. They don't really know who you are or what Uber is—"

"Yet."

"Yet. But there's nothing to really like about taxi. They're not going to do well in a public fight."

He wrote *unsympathetic enemy* on the whiteboard.

"Look, if you were fighting against someone sympathetic—like environmentalists or people who love kittens—"

"Teachers."

"Actually, you can beat the teachers. But anyway, no one likes the taxi industry. We're good there."

"So what else?"

I shrugged. "I think that's pretty much everything. I mean, you wouldn't go to all this trouble if it wasn't really worth it."

"If we have to ask for something that's already legal, we'll never roll out. Not doing this is the same thing as just folding up shop." He wrote *high stakes* on the whiteboard.

I looked at the whiteboard. High stakes. Unsympathetic enemy. Cost of doing business. Legal risks. Typical pols. Local riders/voters. Lots of them.

"Wait," he said. "One thing." He wrote = *beg for forgiveness.*

And that was the formula—the equation that fueled every political fight in Uber's expansion across the United States and around most of the world.

Travis's Law, as it became known, says that in any jurisdiction with the rule of law (meaning where elected officials are democratically chosen by the people), Uber is better off entering the market with or without permission, demonstrating the product to the public, and building a customer base. When regulators then—at the behest of the taxi industry—try to shut Uber down, they turn their riders into advocates and use grassroots political pressure to ensure Uber's continued existence.

What made Travis's Law come together was the unlikely pairing of his instincts and my disillusionment. Travis knew absolutely nothing about politics, but he understood his product and his customers (few as they were back then) in a way no one other than the founder of a startup can. He knew from the reactions he'd gotten from riders and drivers in San Francisco and New York that people would be not only willing to use Uber but to fight for it. He didn't have any focus groups or polling or consumer surveys to base that on. He just knew.

But the other half may have been even more unusual. After nearly twenty years working on campaigns and for politicians, I knew too much to maintain faith in the system. I was lucky to have worked for some exceptional people, but by and large, what drove the system was not the flow of ideas and public policy. Not the genuine desire to look at the landscape of concepts and choose what's best for the public. Not even a basic willingness to consider risking an election in order to make a tough vote (or even put forward a tough proposal) and get something done. Just need, need, and more need.

Spending more years of my life being derivative of someone else and working around the clock to help fill the holes in their psyches

IF YOU'RE A STARTUP

TRYING TO DECIDE WHETHER TO ASK FOR PERMISSION OR BEG FOR FORGIVENESS

 What's the jurisdiction? Are the regulators and electeds corrupt or can you work with them?

 Can you count on grassroots support from customers?

 How compelling is your narrative?

 What are the existing laws on the books?

 Whom are you begging for forgiveness? (3 years in jail is a lot different than a $300 fine)

 What are the political strengths of your opponents?

 How important is this? (Do you have to win no matter what?)

wasn't something I was willing to do anymore. But that didn't mean suddenly changing careers and becoming an orthodontist. I still loved politics. And I'd learned far too much—good and bad—over the years not to put it to use.

Travis's Law offered the ultimate use case—take every lesson I'd learned about what motivates politicians and drives public policy and use it to help startups like Uber fight off political attacks from entrenched interests who didn't want competition.

At the time, I didn't realize this would become the foundation for all of our work around tech and politics. I just thought it was a good idea. How little I knew.

15

Mobilizing Lots of Customers Defeats Conventional Wisdom

Just because plenty of taxi medallion owners are lazy and corrupt doesn't mean they didn't put up a fight. In fact, because their messaging was so similar in market after market and their tactics were so similar (pressuring regulators to issue cease and desist orders to Uber), we thought they must have been coordinating illegally. So much so that we hired David Boies* to look into whether we had an antitrust case worth making in Washington. (His firm's conclusion was that taxi was so disorganized, so local, and so insular that despite seeing the same type of opposition in each market, they weren't sophisticated enough to actually collude.)

But taxi had their allies and none were stronger than Ron Linton. Linton ran the Washington, D.C., Taxicab Commission. Anyone who's

---

* This was before anyone knew about Boies's role in the Harvey Weinstein scandal.

ever taken a taxi in our nation's capital knows they probably have the worst taxi system of any city, anywhere. The zone pricing system makes no sense. Sometimes they'll randomly force you to share a cab with strangers. The cabs themselves are really old, in really bad shape, and frequently unsafe. Street hails were a gamble so you never knew if you'd get a cab or not. And like in most cities, taxis were frequently reluctant to pick up people of color or to drive to low-income neighborhoods. If any city needed Uber, it was D.C.

Not according to Linton. Uber threatened his empire, threatened everything he held dear. And at the behest of Linton and the taxi industry, Councilwoman Mary Cheh introduced legislation to effectively ban Uber from operating in D.C. Of course, the proposed legislation didn't specifically ban Uber. It just set Uber's minimum fare as five times that of a taxi, essentially making it unaffordable. And for good measure, it also prohibited digital dispatch, prohibited use of an iPhone to determine the length and cost of the trip, required drivers to be able to provide a printed receipt for passengers (email somehow was much less useful than a random scrap of paper), and so on.

At that point, Travis's Law was a concept more than a reality. We knew our riders were passionate. We knew they'd probably fight for Uber if asked. But their main job is to use the service, not act as our lobbyists. So igniting what Travis called "rolling thunder" was something we didn't take lightly. But in this case, Cheh's bill was headed for easy passage and a quick signature by the mayor. Why wouldn't it? The local taxi regulator was telling them to do it. Their donors from the taxi industry were demanding it. Uber was this small startup from San Francisco. All conventional political logic dictated you take care of your donors ahead of some company based three thousand miles away.

Except Linton, Cheh, and the city council got the math wrong. They didn't factor in the one entity they're supposed to care about in the first place: their constituents.

We created a Twitter hashtag: #UberDCLove. We put out a press release that the city council was trying to force Uber from D.C. Then Travis sent all our D.C. customers an email titled "Un-independence" to let them know what was happening.

"It was hard for us to believe that an elected body would choose to keep prices of a transportation service artificially high—but the goal is essentially to protect a taxi industry that has significant experience in influencing local politicians," he wrote. "They want to make sure there is no viable alternative to a taxi in Washington D.C., and so on Tuesday, the D.C. city council is going to formalize that principle into law." He then asked for help, not only encouraging each customer to speak out but providing the phone numbers, email addresses, and Twitter handles for every member of the city council.

Did they ever. Fifty thousand emails. Thirty-seven thousand tweets. In three days. The council panicked. A contentious issue for them typically meant a few dozen calls and emails and few, if any, tweets. Sure, doing the bidding of their donors in the taxi industry was just business as usual, but that type of pay-to-play politics works a lot better in secret. Most constituents don't notice what happens in government, so for most politicians, if they can take care of their supporters, keep the campaign cash coming in, and no one's really the wiser, great. But this time, they touched the third rail. Their constituents hated the taxi system. They were desperate for a better alternative. Uber finally offered them what they wanted, and now their own elected officials were going to take it away?*

Cheh saw the wave of anger and objection and quickly shelved her

---

* The *Washington Post* captured it perfectly in a column about the fight, ending with, "In other words, the system worked. Through rigorous public participation, grievances were redressed in a mutually agreeable manner that protects diverse interests. Woo, democracy." Woo, democracy indeed.

bill. None of her colleagues wanted to touch it. (At that point, proposing the creation of a leper colony in the middle of Union Station might have been more popular.) We wrote new legislation authorizing Uber in D.C.—the Public Vehicle-for-Hire Innovation Amendment Act (legalizing digital dispatch, allowing fares to be charged based on time and distance, setting standards for price transparency, and creating a single licensing system for taxis and Ubers). It passed later that year. Unanimously. Even the sponsors of the anti-Uber legislation voted for it.

The D.C. fight confirmed everything we needed to know: Just like Uber was seriously disrupting the status quo in the taxi industry itself, we could disrupt the status quo of governing too. Calling entrenched interests out on corruption and pay-to-play politics wasn't new. Using your own app to mobilize your customers to swamp their elected officials with complaints was. This would prove to be the thesis behind dozens of campaigns we've run for startups ever since.

16

Thank You, Bill de Blasio

Of course, nothing's ever easy. Similar problems started cropping up all over the country. In Massachusetts, taxi tried to get both local and state government to shut us down. (It didn't work.) In Pennsylvania, they tried to do their dirty work through the Philadelphia Parking Authority. (We stopped them.) In Denver, they went through the Colorado Public Utilities Commission. (Stopped them again.) In Chicago, the taxi commissioner was a holdover from the Richard M. Daley administration, which was the Illinois bastion of pay-to-play politics. (I was more than a little familiar with it.) She desperately tried to keep Uber out of the market, but fortunately Rahm had become mayor, liked innovation, and realized his voters wanted the ability to use Uber, so he shut her down. In Los Angeles, they tried to keep us out of the airport.

We had skirmishes in Seattle, Montreal, and Houston. Taxi had some success, at least short term, in Las Vegas and Miami, where the governing systems were so complex and multijurisdictional that turning the people's ire on any one bad guy was a lot harder. Eventually though, we got through in both cities.

As we won the right to operate in city after city, the company took off. It turned out that people hated their local taxi system everywhere. And once Travis launched UberX, allowing anyone to use their own car to give someone else a ride, the business really exploded. It needed more than me and a few of my employees handling the political stuff. It was time to build a real, internal team. And once we did, around a year later, we stopped working directly for Uber. They had what they needed in-house. I still gave advice to Travis on a variety of issues (given the rapidly growing value of my equity, I was as economically and emotionally invested as anyone could be), but my involvement waned, and I wanted to replicate what we did for Uber with other startups.

But I couldn't. Other startups weren't Uber. Other founders weren't Travis. I'd go talk to a founder, explain the regulatory problems coming at them, explain my background and expertise, say we'd work for equity and he'd typically respond along the lines of: "You don't understand. I went to Stanford. I was in Y Combinator. Kleiner led our Series A. John Doerr is on our board. When those stupid regulators see how smart I am, they'll just do whatever we want."

I'd try to explain that politics didn't really work that way, but they rarely listened. Because so many startup founders have engineering backgrounds, they're incredibly logical in some ways, but very obtuse in others. They have inputs that matter in their world: fund-raising, user acquisition, growth, deployment of new features on the platform. Politicians have inputs that matter in their world: fund-raising, poll numbers, press coverage. Founders, at least in theory, look at the world as capitalists. Dollars and cents are how they ultimately judge their success or failure. (Although some startups are allowed to lose money for so long, the notion of profitability gets away from them.) Politicians judge their success by elections.

So even if everything is logical and right to a startup and there's no good reason why a politician should oppose them, the politician isn't looking at it that way. He or she thinks, "How does this impact my donors? How does this play with the different interest groups whose support I need? How does this play in the press? How will this impact my favorability and approval rating?"

If you can think about and reframe your issue in that context—if a politician thinks that denying your right to operate will hurt him on election day—then you can convince most politicians to do just about anything.

The problem wasn't that startups needed to take politics more seriously. And the problem wasn't figuring out how to influence politicians and regulators so they'll do what you want. (We knew how to do that.) The problem was convincing a typically very self-confident, often arrogant breed of founders that they had to invest time, money, and equity in preventing and solving political problems.

Maybe I'm just not a good salesman but I couldn't get the point across to most of them. And then finally, we got lucky. Bill de Blasio did it for me.

In the four hours from when Travis first called to ask for help till my flight landed at LaGuardia, I'd put together a game plan. As I sat there on the plane, I realized that de Blasio's perception of Uber and the reality of Uber were two very different things. Because de Blasio was so indifferent—even hostile—to tech, he only knew of Uber as the startup that raised a ton of money and had the black Suburbans lined up on Park Avenue. Sure, that was part of Uber's business, but not everything. Our drivers, I thought, are almost all immigrants and minorities looking to make more money than they could driving a cab or working another job. Our customers numbered plenty of millennials, but also a lot of working people who lived in the boroughs and used UberX because it was cheaper and more convenient than taking a taxi, and for black and Latino customers (much of de Blasio's base), the experience of being passed over by an empty taxi once the driver saw the color of their skin had created decades of deep-seated resentment. No one knows the color of your finger when you summon an Uber, so to many New Yorkers, taxis were the bad guys and Uber represented real, positive change.

By the time my flight reached cruising altitude, it hit me that the fight to kill de Blasio's proposal of capping Uber's growth at 1 percent a year would work a lot better if we ran the campaign from his left. He'd never faced that before. (No one had ever thought they could question his progressive bona fides.) Reacting to it would mean coming up with a new playbook on the fly. We could try to catch him by surprise, co-opt everyone who normally sided with him because they didn't want to be seen as illiberal, and create enough chaos to at least put quick passage of the bill in question.

The other weapon we had was de Blasio's motivation—calling it corrupt would be an insult to the corrupt. At the time, de Blasio wasn't seen as that crooked. But the taxi medallion owners were his second-biggest donors. And they hated Uber. They had deep pockets, but the value of their taxi medallions (once priced as high as $1.3 million each) was plummeting as riders chose Uber in droves.

We later learned that several major taxi medallion owners wrote the legislation and handed it to de Blasio, who promptly had it introduced in the city council. But at the time, we just knew that taxi would do what they always do—leverage their campaign donations to try to get politicians to protect them from competition. We also knew that just as they'd never bothered to improve their product or service, they probably wouldn't mount an effective campaign in support of the legislation. The mayor's motives were suspect at best—and that was useful ammunition for us.

But as Mike Tyson said, "everyone has a plan until they get punched in the face." The ideas that made sense in theory on an airplane somewhere over the southeastern United States weren't necessarily the ideas that'd translate into success in downtown Manhattan.

I headed over to Uber's NYC headquarters first thing the next morning. When I started working with Uber, their New York office was basically a large closet in Long Island City, Queens. Things had changed. The new office employed around a hundred people, was in far West Chelsea, one of the hippest parts of Manhattan, and looked exactly like what you'd imagine the stereotypical startup-gone-very-rich space would look like.

Josh Mohrer, Uber's longtime and extremely successful general manager of New York (and now one of my partners at Tusk Ventures), met me at the door. I wasn't expecting the team assembled—high-level Uber execs from across the country were there, ready to take on the fight. Travis mentioned how problematic it'd be globally for Uber if the bill passed, but the presence of Rachel Holt, who ran operations for North America, Justin Kintz, who ran policy and politics across North America, Matt McKenna, who helped run the communications shop, and a bunch of others made it abundantly clear how worried they were about this.

"This isn't just New York," Rachel told me as we sat down. "The same idea has already popped up in London and Mexico City. If we stop it here, the idea probably dies everywhere. If it happens here, we could be fucked everywhere."

Her analysis made sense. New York City is the global media capital of the world. It's the opposite of Vegas—what happens in New York is seen everywhere. It's why AT&T hired us to figure out how to get Jon Stewart to stop attacking them in his opening monologue. (His complaints were about AT&T's service locally but it gave the company a bad name globally.) It's why the lack of being legal in New York drove the

Ultimate Fighting Championship crazy. It wasn't that they lost that much revenue from not hosting events at Madison Square Garden, it was that regulators across the world knew they were illegal in New York and that created problems everywhere. (It took years, but we eventually helped get it done.) It also turned out to be a major problem for Airbnb, who passed on the opportunity to reach a data-sharing agreement with Eric Schneiderman, the New York State attorney general, an ill-fated decision that first led to legislation effectively banning Airbnb's model in New York and then turned into regulatory problems everywhere from Southampton to Singapore. The risk for Uber was severe and they knew it.

When Travis said "whatever you need," we took it seriously. Melissa Heuer from my team began drawing up paid media budgets—TV, radio, direct mail, digital—as well as what we'd need for phones, grassroots, polling, lobbying, legal, and everything else a well-funded campaign could possibly require.

At first blush, it seemed to me we had two paths: (1) surprise city hall by attacking from the left, and/or (2) take our argument to the U.S. attorney's office that this was pure, pay-to-play corruption, and if they agreed and started looking into it, that might convince city hall to back off before they got themselves in serious trouble.

On the one hand, this was all really exciting. The stakes were high. The fight was going to be extremely public—covered by all the papers and all media, local, national, and global every day. We were on the side of the angels. We had as much money as we needed. Having a combination like that is very rare. On the other hand, the playing field couldn't have been much worse. Why would twenty-six members of the council turn on the mayor to help a startup? Normally, they never would. So we had to make the political consequences of voting against Uber even more painful than voting against the mayor.

We assembled an all-star team of half a dozen local lobbying firms to focus on each individual member of the council. Our team wasn't quite as extensive as Pharma's legendary operation in D.C., which has more lobbyists than there are members of Congress, but it had to be a record for city government.

We met for the first time that week and went through the roll call. It was grim. Not only did we have less than half a dozen votes on our side lined up, the vote on the bill itself was scheduled to happen in just a few weeks. City hall was trying to railroad it through.

We split the strategy into two components: (1) generate massive public opposition to the bill through TV ads, radio ads, banner ads, rallies, newspaper support, pundit support, clergy support, community support, driver support, and support from elected officials (the outside game), and (2) conduct an intense lobbying campaign to somehow line up twenty-six No votes in the council, constituting a constant barrage of calls, emails, and tweets from constituents, direct mail in each district either praising the councilmember for opposing the bill or attacking him or her for supporting it, polling to show the bill was unpopular, and having our team of lobbyists suffocate each member and their staffs (the inside game).

We hit the airwaves fast: drivers—immigrants and people of color mainly—asking why de Blasio was trying to take away their livelihood. Jimmy Siegel and Miriam Hess made the ads—they're geniuses at capturing real people and putting snippets together into a compelling narrative—and this spot made de Blasio's worst nightmare come true: He looked right-wing, anti-immigrant, antiminority, and corrupt, all at once. We put over a thousand points behind the ad and blasted it out everywhere. That meant we were spending well over $1 million per week to air the spot, and the press went crazy with it, magnifying the impact tenfold.

At that point, it should have dawned on team de Blasio that this was a really dumb fight for them for a few key reasons:

- The mayor's attack was coming from the wrong place. When you have a policy position and it's motivated by true policy goals, then even if you're wrong, people will usually respect you for believing in something and fighting for it. In this case, the attack was coming solely as an attempt to take care of donors: donors who happen to be particularly sleazy.

- The attack didn't mesh with de Blasio's overall agenda. His entire mayoralty was based on a narrative of *A Tale of Two Cities*. It was him and lower-income New Yorkers versus the rich. That narrative works because it squarely aligns him with his base. But in this case, the Uber ban would have hurt both drivers (the vast majority of whom were immigrants and minorities) and taken away a solution to taxi's long history of racism. That's why our second ad featured riders from the outer reaches of Brooklyn, Queens, and the Bronx who talked about being ignored by yellow taxi after yellow taxi because of the color of their skin. That literally can't happen with Uber, so de Blasio was on the wrong side of something his base felt on a truly visceral level.

- The bill meant little to de Blasio. He didn't care about taxis one way or another and even he didn't buy his own argument that Uber was the cause of congestion in New York City. He just wanted to take care of his donors. But for Uber, the bill meant everything. If the most visible and important city in the world put a hard cap on Uber's growth, taxi would try the same thing everywhere. That meant a disproportionate willingness to spend capital and resources. Uber would throw anything it had to at the fight. There was no chit not worth calling in, no dollar not worth spending. It meant we went to bed thinking about this and we woke up thinking about this—and they didn't. That allowed us to run circles around them throughout the campaign.*

- Our narrative was a lot better than theirs. We had jobs, ethics, minority rights, immigrant rights, and innovation all on our side. They just had this absurd claim about congestion. If they had a more compelling argument, they probably could have held on to the votes in the council and pushed the bill through. But when you're solely acting on the behest of donors (which is frequently the case for proposed antitech legislation and regulations), you can get away with it until someone calls you out on it and devotes the resources to making it painful.

- They had no real-world support. There were no real people who cared about their side—they just had the taxi owners. While Uber's image took a severe beating in 2017, at the time, we were the good guys. And we had an army of two million customers in New York City and fifty thousand drivers. Yes, there's a reason they say, "You can't fight city hall." But if you have to, having the numbers on your side goes a long way.

- We also had a way to mobilize our supporters: the app. Once people are already inside your app, quickly explaining an issue to them and then making it easy for them to advocate on your behalf by pressing a few buttons is a major advantage. The Uber app in New York City is opened hundreds of thousands of times every

---

* This is an important thing for every startup to remember. Yes, the regulators and politicians have a lot more power than you do. But they're also dealing with a million different issues at once and your problem has only so much meaning to them. That means that you're likely to be far more focused on the outcome than they are and that offers a competitive advantage in any campaign.

day. And when Kaitlin Durkosh on the Uber New York team had the brilliant idea of making "de Blasio" one of the options on the app (next to Uber Black, UberX, UberXL, etc.), we had a way to capture people and mobilize them. (If you chose the de Blasio option, you were told there was a twenty-five-minute wait time, we explained the problem, and then asked people to email and tweet at their councilmembers to tell them to oppose the bill. In a week, over 250,000 did.)

The lobbyists took a lot of shit from both city hall (who tried to convince each lobbyist to drop Uber as a client by threatening harm to their other clients) and from the council (none of them liked suddenly being called out in a very public way for supporting the bill). But to their credit, they all hung in there, and as we held whip count calls multiple times each day, the number of No votes slowly started to increase. And the more that some members were willing to publicly oppose the bill, the easier it became for others to follow suit. None of them said to themselves, "This bill is wrong and stupid, I'm being called out in front of my constituents for supporting it, I'm getting called, emailed, and tweeted at constantly, every good lobbyist in the city is all over me to oppose the bill, and the newspapers are all against the bill, but I'm still going to take a beating for de Blasio anyway." Truly great leaders can sometimes pull that off—but only if they've developed a lot of goodwill with the legislature and taken their share of hits for them. Most councilmembers considered de Blasio to be aloof, patronizing, condescending, and selfish, so none were all that eager to suffer for his sins.

Getting the *Times* was a big turning point. Neither the *New York Post* nor the *New York Daily News* were huge fans of the mayor, so while we appreciated the support from their editorials and columnists, we also counted on it. The *New York Times* was a wild card—they didn't dislike de Blasio as much, they were anticorporation in general, and they didn't have any particular affinity for Uber. But David Plouffe, who ran Obama's 2008 presidential campaign, had joined Uber as the head of government relations a year earlier, was able to go see the *Times* editorial board, and made the case on the merits of the bill itself (or lack thereof), and they, luckily, agreed with him.

The *Daily News* then published a cartoon of de Blasio holding a yellow taxi in one hand and a pile of green cash in another, with the caption "Yellow is My New Green." We saw the cartoon at 5 a.m. By 7:30 we had people holding thousands of copies, handing them out at all of the subway stops near city hall .

And by feeding the frenzy of the press, we kept the pressure on city hall and on the city council. We organized several hundred clergy to meet with us and talk about why the bill was bad for their parishioners and their communities. Plouffe met with Al Sharpton, who voiced his opposition to the bill. Elected officials from around the city started coming out in our favor. Brooklyn Borough President Eric Adams appeared at a driver rally. Bronx Borough President Rubén Díaz Jr. announced his opposition. So did Comptroller Scott Stringer. And Congressman Hakeem Jeffries. At the time, all four men were potential primary challengers to de Blasio, so their opposition allowed the press to start telling the story of the fight in the context of the next election. (Reporters love politics and process and both are far easier to cover and explain than public policy itself, so if you want reporters to focus on something, make it easy for them.)

While everyone from Travis on down was fully supportive of our plan, Uber had become a big company with a lot of chiefs, a board, and offices all over the world. Keeping everyone informed and on the same page wasn't easy. And that's where the 7 a.m. email came in handy.

Every morning, we'd send out a comprehensive account of where everything stood based on our strategic goals: breaking down de Blasio

IF YOU'RE A STARTUP FACING

INACTION FROM REGULATORS WHO DON'T KNOW HOW TO INTERPRET WHAT YOU DO UNDER CURRENT LAW (OR REFUSE TO DO SO)

Why are they stalled? Confusion, regulatory capture, or intransigence?

Is pay-to-play involved?

Do they have a valid reason to delay? Does it open up a can of regulatory / legislative worms?

What will it take to move them? Do you need a big public fight?

If you succeed in moving them, how does it impact other jurisdictions?

(with tactics like TV ads, radio ads, lobbying, grassroots, PR, polling), getting Speaker Melissa Mark-Viverito to pull her support for the bill (same list of tactics plus putting a lot of pressure on her individual members), getting the governor to support us (since he hated de Blasio even more than we did, instigating a rift between the speaker and the mayor was both something he could and would love to do), and exploring legal remedies (suing the law itself as unconstitutional and also pointing out the pay-to-play to U.S. Attorney Preet Bharara office so they'd consider investigating it).

The fight lasted a few weeks. We kept upping the stakes with more

TV, more radio, more calls, more lobbying, more public pressure. City hall asked to meet but when they wouldn't agree to first pull the bill, we said (and then announced publicly) we'd meet only if the meeting were livestreamed so the people could see what this was all about. (The meeting obviously never happened.) We announced we were buying TV time well into August so even if the bill passed, we were going to stay on the air attacking everyone anyway. (Otherwise, making the problem go away by passing the bill as quickly as possible was an appealing option for the council.) Councilmembers kept jumping to our side. But until the speaker decided she too no longer wanted this problem, we knew she could always apply enough pressure to ram the votes through.

Then we got lucky. The mayor, as he is apt to do, deflected blame for the bill by putting it on Mark-Viverito instead. The speaker, of course, had nothing to do with it, and seeing the mayor throw her under the bus was the last straw. She'd had it. She was no longer interested in seeing her members take constant public hits to carry the mayor's water. Then Cuomo came out publicly against the bill. Celebrities like Ashton Kutcher and Kate Upton started tweeting about it. City hall had nowhere to hide. The call came in.

"They want to meet," Josh told me.

"Not if they're still pushing the bill," I said.

"They want to make this go away."

"We can do that—they just need to drop the bill."

The whole team spent the next few hours preparing for the meeting. It was, presumably, a negotiation to drop the bill. They'd want concessions—they'd need cover to make a deal. We made a list. Josh, Rachel, and a few Uber officials and lobbyists went to the meeting. (We decided I was better off playing the bogeyman they could point to in the meeting and say that the deal wasn't good enough and I'd just keep publicly kicking the shit out of the mayor and the council if we couldn't reach the right resolution.) I anxiously waited by my phone for the results.

A text from Josh came in. "All good."

But then nothing for twenty minutes. All good with what? What did that mean? The phone rang. Josh again.

"They pulled the bill."

"What'd we have to give up?"

"Nothing."

"What do you mean nothing?"

"We just promised to end the campaign—take down the TV ads, no more radio ads, no more mail, no more email or tweets."

"That's it?"

"That's it. They just want it to go away."

Turns out you can fight city hall.

We'd won. The coverage reflected that extensively, everywhere. And it showed: Rumors of similar legislative attacks in other cities went away. Mayors considering doing the bidding of their taxi donors thought twice. Travis was thrilled. My team was excited to win such a high-profile fight. And most important (for us), all of the attention around the fight helped other startups realize that they had to start taking politics seriously. Their newly realized challenge was our opportunity. And we took it.

SECTION IV

A New Venture in Venture

17

To Do Big Things, Hire Big Talent (and Pay Them Well)

When Uber was the only startup in our portfolio, the work wasn't anything we couldn't handle with our current team. Multiplying that by twelve or more meant devoting real resources—at least real for me—to the business. (My estimate was around $4 million per year and that turned out to be a little low.) It meant hiring a real investment team who could analyze and negotiate deals. (Getting equity is only useful if the equity will be worth multiples of what you'd get up front in cash, given the risk you're taking and the six- to nine-year typical timeframe to see an early-stage venture investment pay off.)

Unless Uber completely cratered and the value of my equity plummeted, I could afford to take some financial risk. Tusk Strategies was spitting out enough profits every year to absorb the cost of a venture business, although it'd mean giving up a lot of disposable income. I had both the time to focus on something new and, after five years of Tusk Strategies, I was bored and needed a change.

"Fuck it," I finally said to myself. "What do you ever accomplish by being passive and afraid?"

I knew how to help startups solve their political problems. But I had no idea how to pick the right startups to work with. (Uber was just luck.) I had no idea how to do due diligence of them or structure our deals with them. I needed help. Then I met Jordan Nof.

Jordan worked at Blackstone, running their internal venture portfolio. Because venture is usually tiny compared to the types of deals a giant like Blackstone usually funds, Jordan was frustrated by the lack of internal interest in his work. He was ready to take a risk, even if it meant being the head of investments at a firm that didn't even exist yet. That helped. But we needed more.

Matt Yale had been our client at Tusk Strategies. Matt was running government relations, investor relations, and public relations for Laureate, the world's largest higher-education company with over a million students on campuses around the world. Matt and I knew each other in Chicago, he had backed Obama for president, and spent two and a half years at the U.S. Department of Education as one of Arne Duncan's top aides and advisers. He was spending all of his time on a plane, traveling around the world for Laureate. It'd been four years. He was ready for a change.

Jen Hanley served as Hillary's press secretary during the Senate years and while we didn't overlap, I was a little nervous when we met. (Turns out she didn't know or care about my role in fueling the Chuck-Hillary rivalry.) Jen went on to run global communications for KKR, another giant private equity fund. But her husband had just gotten a job in Boston. KKR told her she'd need to commute to New York every day. Even though we had never been a PR firm, I knew that if we were going to ask startups for 1 to 3 percent of their company in exchange for our work, it had to include communications. I didn't care where Jen worked from. I cared about having her on our team. She was ready for a change.

My sister, Marla Tusk, had recently moved to New Jersey after spending years in D.C., first as an attorney in the counterterrorism unit of the Justice Department and then running the appellate division for the U.S. attorney's office of Northern Virginia. Marla was always a lot smarter than me. She was valedictorian of her high school, graduated at the top of her class from Wharton, got a full scholarship to Columbia Law School (and in part, took it to turn down Harvard Law, after turning down Yale for college just to really piss off our mom). She was the editor of the law review, clerked on the Second Circuit, and won multiple awards for her work at Justice. Her husband, Josh, had held a variety of big jobs in business and politics and wanted to move home to New Jersey to run for congress. Marla had two little kids at the time, but was itching to do some kind of work. She was way overqualified to be our general counsel and until now, we had never needed a general counsel. (My rudimentary legal skills were more or less enough.) I never expected her to say yes when I offered her the job, but she was ready for a change.

I had met Marla Kanemitsu close to twenty years earlier when she started dating my friend Mark Moller from law school. She built a very successful career as a defense attorney in insurance law, but when Mark became a professor at DePaul Law School, she kept her job at a law firm in D.C. and was commuting back and forth to Chicago every week. We needed a lot more brainpower on our regulatory team, and since Bob Greenlee was already in Chicago, there was no reason we couldn't build a team there. She was ready for a change.

Bob, who runs our multistate regulatory efforts (and worked with me for Rod, was in my class in law school, and is one of my partners at Tusk Ventures), then hired a lot more people. Jen did too. So did Jordan. Matt built a team. We convinced Seth Webb (from both the Parks and

Blagojevich days) to leave his job as town manager of Killington, Vermont, and join us. Every time we added someone else to the payroll, my dad, Gabe, who is the CFO of Tusk Holdings, gulped hard. I was taking almost all of our profit margin at Tusk Strategies and using it to staff up Tusk Ventures. But it was my money, and if my dad had learned one thing about me over time, it was that I was going to do what I thought made sense.

But what actually did make sense? While the fights Uber, Airbnb, and other startups faced helped founders realize they had to take politics seriously, and while we were unquestionably the best (and probably only) people equipped to anchor the intersection of tech and politics, it's still hard to convince a startup to give you a chunk of their company without getting a check in return. And even if we could, picking the right startups is incredibly difficult. Uber is a needle in the haystack. To generate at least a 3x return, we'd need to pick a lot of winners, which meant we'd need to convince a lot of startups to hire us. We'd need to take a lot of risk and accept a lot of unknowns.

"Why can't someone just copy us?" my dad asked.

"They could. But if you're someone like me who comes out of politics and starts a consulting firm, your goal is to build it up for five to ten years and then sell it to a giant holding company like WPP or Omnicom. If you do that, you can't do this. Their model doesn't fit an equity for services approach."

"You're the only one who never sold?"

"No, of course not. But let's say you're me, even if you never had any interest in working for some giant company, to do this, you'd still need a lot of other things to pull this off."

"Like?"

"Like the cash flow. We can only afford to do this because Tusk Strategies makes enough money to cover the costs of running Tusk Ventures. And because I can forgo savings because of my Uber stock."

"You're the only rich political consultant? And why do you even need to do this? The Uber money is more than you need."

"But that's what gives us the freedom to take the risk. And it's why people are unlikely to copy us: You have to have a pretty high risk tolerance to take most of your profits and reinvest them in startups. And you have to be bored and anxious enough to want to keep doing more things rather than just sitting on a beach somewhere. Most people aren't that crazy."

"And if someone else is?"

"Even then, they need the expertise to get the clients and do the work. What are our two big credentials here? Uber, the most successful startup in the world, and Mike Bloomberg, the single most successful person to work in both tech and politics. No one else has that. And even if they did, what makes Tusk Ventures work is the same model that makes Tusk Strategies work: We can run big, complicated campaigns in lots of places at once."

"And if you pick the wrong startups?"

"I'm sure we will. But we'll also put a sixty-day out in every contract so when it becomes clear we picked wrong, we can get out. Our only cost is our time."

I couldn't really articulate that my ego, my insecurity, and my appetite for change and ideas and a constant flow of new stuff all demanded more than just banking my Uber profits and running a nice, small, profitable consulting firm. But he's my dad, so he probably understood all that already.

In fact, I think I saw him smile as he walked away.

18

Don't Confuse Ideology with Politics

On August 3, 2015, thanks to my friend and PR genius Stu Loeser, the *Times* ran a story about how Uber's political adviser was launching a firm to help startups solve problems in return for equity. It wasn't long before the phone started ringing, and with Handy, one of our first clients, we learned quickly that this business wasn't going to be a cakewalk.

Handy is a platform that connects consumers to housekeepers and handymen. The premise is pretty simple: People have paid other people to clean their homes for thousands of years. And yet even today, housekeeping operates mainly in the gray economy. Most of it is off the books. There's little regulation. Few taxes are paid. There is no systematic way for people to find a good housekeeper or for housekeepers to find work.

And as more and more people kept changing the way they work, being able to offer services on the Handy platform for five or ten hours a week while they're in college or taking care of an elderly relative or transitioning to a new career made a lot of sense. Oisin Hanrahan founded Handy when he was still in business school at Harvard. He and his cofounder, Umang Dua, built the platform and started recruiting people from both sides of the equation—customers and housekeepers/handymen.

It worked. Handy quickly attracted serious venture funding, raising $50 million from funds like General Catalyst, Revolution, and TPG. They launched in New York and quickly expanded to other cities in the United States like Boston, Chicago, Los Angeles, San Francisco, Denver, Houston, Seattle, and so on, as well as into Canada and the UK. And then the problems started.

Handy's professionals (the term for cleaners and handymen) are independent contractors. U.S. labor law divides workers into two categories: independent contractors and full-time employees. Full-time employees receive benefits and get Social Security, and their work is their main profession. Independent contractors typically work for a variety of different people part-time, so they're self-employed. The law has a variety of tests to determine when someone is a full-time employee and when someone is an independent contractor, but it varies by state and is frequently, and deliberately, very vague.

Why would anyone want to make it hard to figure out what the law is and how to comply with it? Yep. Politics.

Imagine you're a labor union. You hate independent contractors—you can't organize them, you can't represent them, and most important, you can't charge them dues. If the law gives clear, firm guidance to businesses as to what constitutes full-time employment and what constitutes independent contractor status, then everyone has to live by it. Seems fair, right? Not if you want to rig the outcome. Vague laws mean more opportunity for regulators to interpret them however they want.

So if you're a politically powerful union who donates millions of dollars to political candidates and conducts extensive get-out-the-vote operations on Election Day, vague laws plus political influence mean lots of adjudications against businesses who work with independent contractors. It means state labor departments are told by the governor's office (who appoints the labor commissioner) to interpret the vague state laws in the way the union wants, every time.

Enter the sharing economy. Every sharing-economy platform—whether it's Uber, Lyft, Handy, Postmates, DoorDash, Instacart, or anything else—is predicated on the notion that people who want to perform a service are connected via the platform to people who need the service. The platform's job is to put the parties together, facilitate the transaction, and take a fee in return. The platform is not meant to be the provider of the services nor the employer of the people providing the services.

If sharing-economy platforms are deemed by regulators to be full-time employers, the business models don't really work (at least in most cases). And that's typically labor's goal: stop the growth of the sharing economy before it attracts more and more people.

Oisin had a radical idea: Give sharing-economy workers benefits. His view was that our labor laws were wildly outdated. (The federal rules creating the independent contractor/full-time employee system were written in 1938.) Modern life and the modern economy means that people don't spend their careers in one job—they do lots of different things, both over the course of their lives and also frequently all at once. In his view, anyone offering cleaning or handyman services on the Handy platform were clearly independent contractors, setting their own hours and deciding, on a case-by-case basis, whether to accept or turn down any job offered. But why should that preclude them from getting health care? Disability? Workers comp? A pension?

Handy would pay into a portable benefits fund that provided extra money for people to use on any type of benefit they wanted. Any platform participating in the program can pay into the fund, the contractor could choose to also match the amount with pretax money, and it'd be a way to bring benefits to millions of people. For platforms like Handy, being able to offer benefits—without triggering a ruling from every state labor department whose governor relies on union political support that the platform is a full-time employer—meant being able to recruit better contractors to the platform and to incentivize them to choose jobs on the Handy platform.

On its face, who says no? Companies want to give money and benefits to workers who otherwise wouldn't have them—especially in a field like housekeeping that has always operated in the gray economy. It should be Elizabeth Warren's Christmas, Hanukkah, and Kwanzaa wrapped into one, right? Of course not. Because if you can have both the total flexibility of being an independent contractor and setting your own schedule and still get benefits, why join a union and pay dues? So we were faced with an oxymoronic dynamic: private companies wanting to give benefits to workers but unable to because unions wouldn't allow it.

Oisin emailed me, asking to talk. Once he explained his predicament and his idea, it wasn't hard to grasp the challenge: How do you pass proworker legislation over the objections of unions who control the legislature and heavily influence governors?

Handy's key markets—New York, Los Angeles, Chicago, San Francisco—all were housed in Democratic-controlled states. We could try to change their labor laws, but given organized labor's outsized political influence in each state, it was an uphill fight at best. We needed friendly terrain where we could establish the concept, demonstrate it worked, and then use our success to argue for change in more hostile terrain.

We started in Arizona: a state with relatively little union political influence, a tech-friendly governor and legislature, and a market just big enough to matter (Phoenix). Since the labor laws are different in every state, in Arizona, we didn't need a full suite of changes. We just needed clarity in their labor laws that the sharing economy is meant for independent contractors, not full-time workers. We needed a political body to affirm, in writing, what everyone already knew—and what the sharing economy already was. Most campaigns are difficult. This one wasn't: The inside game worked, our lobbyist got the amendment through, and we had our test case.

Oisin is like a lot of startup CEOs. He asks for the sun, the stars, and the moon and then gets upset when the rest of the galaxy isn't thrown in on the house. In other words, he's a very ambitious dude.

"We need to get New York next," he said.

I shook my head. "Tough one. You've got a governor in Cuomo who eats, breathes, and sleeps politics. He's not going to see any political upside in upsetting the unions just to help the sharing economy."

"So can't you just do what you did for Uber? Get everyone riled up and use that to force it through?"

It's not easy to tell the founder of his company that his customers aren't likely to rally to his defense. The demand for Handy's services was strong. But are people truly passionate about being able to secure a housekeeper or electrician on demand? Not really. Fortunately, Oisin was pragmatic enough to accept that. But that just meant we needed to try something else.

Marla Kanemitsu was our point person on Handy. "We need some unions to back us," she argued.

She was right. But it wasn't easy. Marla and Brian Miller (Handy's extremely capable general counsel) started working with Andy Stern, the former president of SEIU International who had taken an interest in the potential of the sharing economy to help people like housekeepers.

They found an ally in Jim Conigliaro Jr., the head of the Machinists

Union in New York. Jim liked the idea of giving benefits to workers who'd otherwise have none. Jim, for a time, was able to bring along the Retail Workers, the Transportation Workers, and the Plumbers. But not 32BJ.

SEIU 32BJ represents security guards and janitors. They don't represent housekeepers. But they saw anything in the cleaning sector as their turf and they were going to protect it no matter what. We went back and forth with them, meeting time and again to show them that all we wanted was to give benefits to people who currently didn't have them and were never going to become 32BJ members in the first place. (Organizing housekeepers, who work almost entirely in the gray economy, is basically impossible.) Why would they object?

If you've been reading this book even half awake, you already know the answer: politics. Héctor Figueroa, 32BJ's president, was essentially no different from any politician. He knew who voted in union elections, who made noise, who caused trouble. If he was willing to engage with businesses in new ways, all that'd bring him was risk. (In fact, Andy Stern lost his role at SEIU for trying to reach agreements on big issues with businesses, alienating the left flank of his membership in the process.) Working with Handy meant clarifying New York's independent contractor laws. That'd mean potentially weakening labor's grip over defining who was and wasn't a full-time employee. Anyone looking to take him out in the next union election would seize on that. Sure, he could argue he helped deliver benefits to tens of thousands of people who currently didn't have them, but let's not be naïve. The mission isn't helping workers. The mission is protecting and maintaining the system.

We took a shot at Cuomo anyway. My friend Jamie Rubin had recently become the state's COO, reporting directly to the governor. Jamie came to government from the business world. (We met when I ran a campaign related to one of his private equity investments.) His political worldview was shaped by the Clinton centrism that his dad, Bob Rubin, helped create during the 1990s. And more important than anything else, he made decisions based on logic, rather than politics.

We went to see him. Convincing Jamie that allowing companies to offer benefits and giving companies clear rules on worker classification wasn't that hard: Anyone not solely looking at the world through only a political lens could see the proposal made sense. But even his own team wasn't on board.

"What does 32BJ think of this?" Elizabeth de Leon, who covered labor issues for the governor's office, asked.

We explained the issue again. And again. She clearly got it. But conceiving of a world where they'd do something over the objections of any powerful union wasn't possible. Sure, we had support from a few unions, but none nearly as powerful as 32BJ. She said she'd get back to us. She never did. Jamie eventually left the governor's office, frustrated with the limitations politics placed on getting things done. We needed a different route.

No one ever thinks, *I want to get something big and complicated done in a relatively short period of time. I'll try to get an Act of Congress.* Our whole thesis was that you can move issues in cities and states where you'd just get stuck forever in the morass of Washington, D.C. But what if the politics make state government an impossible route?

Marla Kanemitsu studied the federal tax laws around worker classification. "In theory, we could amend them so that the people who work on sharing-economy platforms are clearly considered independent contractors."

"This is a law that's been around since FDR. You want to run a campaign to change it? In Washington, D.C.? In this political climate?"

"Well, aren't the Republicans talking about tax reform?"

"They always talk about tax reform. That's what Republicans do."

"But you've got a Republican majority in the House. And the Senate. And a Republican in the White House."

"I'm not sure he's really that type of Republican."

"His whole shtick is being rich. If Congress wants to cut taxes, he's not going to say no." She had a point.

"So write an amendment to the tax code, try to stick it into the broader tax bill, and see what happens?"

She nodded. "It's worth a shot."

Marla started drafting legislation and hired a lobbying firm in D.C. called Capitol Tax Partners to help us round up support. They started surveying the staffs of members of key Republicans and soon found an enthusiastic ally in John Thune, the chairman of the Senate Commerce Committee. We knew that we weren't going to pass a standalone bill on worker classification, but if tax reform did move, Thune clearly had the juice in the Senate to get his amendment included in the bill.

Now we needed the House. According to our lobbyists, we needed a sponsor who sat on the Committee on Ways and Means. And according to the lobbyists, everyone liked our idea but no one wanted to make it their big ask in tax reform. (GOP members of Ways and Means exist to cut taxes so using their chits on anyone else's issue wasn't something they'd take lightly.) Finally, after months of meetings, Congressman Tom Rice from South Carolina signed on as our House sponsor.

Two good sponsors isn't enough to pass anything. So we added another front to the war. Matt Yale knew Matt Rhoades, who had served as Romney's campaign manager in 2012. Matt Rhoades created a PR firm called Definers that specialized in conservative media. While no Republican was likely to take their marching orders from the 32BJs of the world and oppose our idea, they needed positive reinforcement just like everyone else. Even once we got our House sponsor, at a certain point, the bill and all of its amendments was going to end up being debated behind closed doors during reconciliation (the process where the House and Senate try to agree on everything so they can actually pass a law). If our idea didn't have more than one champion in Thune, even if no one disagreed with us, we wouldn't necessarily survive the process. Luckily, Oisin and Brian quickly saw the value and agreed to let us hire them.

Obviously, Handy wasn't the only startup who cared about worker-classification reform. Uber jumped in on our side. Amazon did too. Most of the other major sharing-economy platforms were willing to join conference calls and hear what we were up to, but less willing to devote dollars to help us push the idea over the finish line. They're lucky Handy was so dead set on making this happen either way; they could coast behind Oisin and reap the benefits too.

When the House released their tax plan, we weren't in it. Not good. Apparently, so many members wanted to offer amendments that Kevin Brady, the Ways and Means chairman, just cut the whole thing off. We did better in the Senate, getting in the bill during the second round of amendments. Things were looking good. We were blitzing Republican members of both chambers through lobbying, grassroots outreach, and lots of conservative media. Thune's staff seemed optimistic. And the White House wasn't getting in the way.

Then disaster struck. My phone rang. Marla K.

"The Senate parliamentarian took our amendment out of the bill."

"What? Why? How?"

"She said that it violates the Byrd rule."

"What the fuck is the Byrd rule?"

"In a bill being handled through reconciliation, it means that if an amendment to the bill has a budgetary impact, it can't be included."

"We didn't think about this till now?"

"We did. Our lobbyists confirmed with Thune's staff it'd be fine."

"So what happened?"

"The parliamentarian is a holdover from Harry Reid. She found cover to take out a few amendments that Democrats really don't like. We were one of them."

We went through every possible fix but none of them worked. The tax bill passed at the end of 2017 without us.

But you keep fighting. Sometimes you can construct a really smart campaign and make something happen in a few months. But usually, it's just a mix of constant creativity and persistence. We're working multiple angles to get this done federally. And we're working on legislation and rules in thirteen more states too, with success coming fairly quickly in the low-hanging fruit of Kentucky, Iowa, Tennessee, Indiana, and Utah (and medium-hanging fruit like Florida). Politics isn't rocket science—it's mainly hard work, common sense, and a little creativity. In other words, you just keep going.

19

Make Sure You See It Coming

ven though ESPN's Don Van Natta Jr. covers sports and not tech, his piece on FanDuel and DraftKings's regulatory saga included a quote that succinctly sums up the greatest political risk—and the most important political lesson—facing every startup: "We never saw it coming."

In the immortal words of Pericles, just because you don't take an interest in politics doesn't mean politics won't take an interest in you. You don't even need to go back thousands of years to understand his point: Just like every startup wants to disrupt and reinvent their industry through better ideas and better technology, everyone being disrupted wants to push back through better political connections. You can't eat the world without pissing people off, and FanDuel and

DraftKings, up until the shit hit the fan, either didn't understand this or just didn't care.*

FanDuel and DraftKings—new platforms where sports fans could set lineups of players for each major sport and win or lose money depending on how those players then perform that night—learned the hard way that just ignoring your opponents' political and regulatory reach is not a real strategy. Both companies were not only—very aggressively and very successfully—disrupting fantasy sports and taking market share away from casinos in general, you couldn't turn on *SportsCenter* without seeing their ads. While their foes tended to be slow and bureaucratic, this wasn't just a case of one or two new companies upending some old companies. Combine sports, gaming, and the Internet and you're going to make a lot of enemies: casinos who control sports betting, existing season-long fantasy sports leagues, left-wing politicians and interest groups who hate gaming, right-wing politicians and interest groups who hate gaming, state attorneys general desperate for attention, and plenty of others. So when both startups started flying too close to the sun, things went bad fast.

Both companies raised hundreds of millions of dollars, saw their usership skyrocket, and were soon locked in a death match. In fact, FanDuel and DraftKings were so consumed with beating each other, they just didn't have the bandwidth to pay attention to anything else. In 2014, the Fantasy Sports Trade Association lobbying budget was $75,000 total. That's enough to get you five to six months of one

---

* There are a lot of ways to approach political resistance from entrenched interests. You can choose to fight in the court of public opinion (earned media, social media, paid media) rather than just inside the hallways of government buildings. You can even choose to wait until your competition comes after you politically—as long as that's a clearly understood, proactive decision that you know exactly how you'll handle once the fight comes. But you cannot just put your head in the sand and hope nothing bad happens.

decent lobbyist in one state. (In other words, it's as if their budget were just zero.)

We had met Christian Genetski, FanDuel's talented general counsel, a few months earlier. KKR is one of FanDuel's biggest investors (they knew us because of Jen), and Ted Oberwager, the partner at KKR handling their venture investments, thought it'd make sense to connect everyone. It was clear to us almost immediately that Christian was extremely smart, savvy, and thoughtful, so we really liked the idea of working with him. He seemed pleased to know that we were more than just the Uber guys, but bringing in someone like us didn't seem essential at the moment.

That all changed on October 5, 2015. The *New York Times* published a stunning accusation, saying that Ethan Haskell, a DraftKings mid-level employee, had used confidential information at DraftKings—information only an employee would have access to—and taken advantage of it to enhance his lineups in a FanDuel competition and win $350,000. (Employees of both startups were banned from playing on their own sites but not on other daily fantasy sites.) While those accusations were never proven, the damage was done: Eric Schneiderman, the New York State attorney general, immediately announced an investigation. Spurred by their local casinos, state lotteries, and everyone else threatened by the explosion of daily fantasy sports, other states soon followed with a variety of criminal and civil inquiries and regulatory investigations, and a media onslaught took place from coast to coast.

The *Times* story flashed across my phone. So did an opportunity. I quickly wrote the following note, unsolicited, to Christian, figuring that either maybe he would now be interested in working with us, or at least we'd provide some useful advice that could win us some goodwill for the future.

"Am sure you're doing all of this already, but if I were you, I'd be doing the following," I wrote. "(1) Make the ban on employee betting permanent (a temporary ban will be an albatross). (2) Hire a very well-known former prosecutor to lead an internal investigation (Eric Holder or Mike Mukasey or someone like that) and develop best practices. (3) Appoint, quickly, an advisory board on ethics and standards loaded with former prosecutors, law professors, and nonprofit leaders who can help implement strong standards and serve as the face of this for you going forward. (4) Write an op-ed for the *Times* acknowledging where things stand, outlining new steps, and making the broader case for legal, regulated fantasy gaming. (5) Make sure your lobbyists in D.C. and each of the states are communicating all of the steps you're taking to legislative leaders, staffers, and governor's office staffers to blunt any immediate reaction. There's more to do than this, and I'm sure you have it covered, but figured I'd pass along a few thoughts just in case."

He wrote back immediately. "When can you start?"

We began working for them that evening. Luckily, the shock of a political onslaught was deep enough to convince everyone at Fan-Duel to green-light all of the measures we were recommending, immediately.

The first thing we did is put together a board of advisers. While most advisory boards are bullshit, in this case, FanDuel not only needed their actual help, they also needed to demonstrate to the broader world that they were taking this seriously. By attaching real adults with real reputations and recognizable names, we'd at least widen the opening to explain fact from fiction and get our story out there. Matt and I started throwing out names.

"Condoleezza Rice," Matt suggested.

"She'd be great," I replied.

"Mary Schapiro? Former head of the SEC?"

"She'd be great. Can't imagine she'd say yes."

"Sally Blount would be good."

"Who is she?"

"Dean of Kellogg. Really brilliant." Matt had gone to business school at Northwestern.

"Tom Ridge?"

"Yes. He'd be good. Solid in every way."

"What about your buddy from baseball?"

"Tim?"

"Yeah, Tim. Brosnan, right?"

"Yep. Former president of MLB. Ran operations there for twenty-five years. He understands the sports business as well as anyone. I'll ask him."

"I've got another one. Terdema Ussery. Was the CEO of the Dallas Mavericks. Really good guy."*

"Cuban's† an investor in DraftKings so assuming they're on good terms, that could work."

"We need some law-enforcement types."

"Michael Garcia would be good."

"Who's Michael Garcia?"

"Used to be the U.S. attorney for the Southern District of New York. Did a great job there. He's a partner now at Kirkland."

"Would he do it? Is he a sports fan?"

"I only know him a bit through politics—his name comes up as a candidate for different offices every so often. I'll call him."

The conversation went on for a while. With Christian's approval,

---

* Ussery was later accused of sexual harassment during his tenure with the Mavs. Turned out to be not such a good guy. This was a few years before #MeToo, but the movement has now changed the way you vet anyone for any role.

† Mark Cuban is the owner of the Mavericks.

Garcia, Ridge, Ussery, and Brosnan all quickly came on board. Christian then hired Debevoise & Plimpton, a prominent white-shoe New York law firm, and that brought us former U.S. attorney general Mike Mukasey to conduct the internal investigation into the Haskell matter.

"The minute trouble starts, you go running for the establishment," Chris Coffey said as he watched us put the pieces together. Of everyone on our team, Chris was the most skeptical of our venture play and most connected to the old guard. (His godfather was Ed Koch, his mother was Koch's chief of staff for twelve years, and Chris worked for Mike Bloomberg in a wide variety of roles before joining us in 2012.) I wanted to tell Chris to go fuck himself but since Chris wins 90-plus percent of the campaigns he runs, it was hard to discount his opinion.

"Why not? If we can leverage their credibility and get their advice, why wouldn't we?"

He smiled. "You should. I would too. But it's not exactly consistent with your disrupting the world rhetoric."

He had a point—but no amount of intellectual honesty was enough to avoid doing what we needed to do to help stop the bleeding.

And bleed we did. Attorneys general in nearly two dozen states launched investigations. The Nevada Gaming Board said that FanDuel and DraftKings were operating illegally and just kicked us out altogether. (There are times to fight and times to let it go; fighting the casinos in Nevada—who control the Gaming Board through and through—is a waste of time and energy.) The legality of daily fantasy sports became an issue in thirty-nine states almost overnight.

We jumped into action. Traditional lobbying was important since the casinos (the real opponent hiding behind left- and right-wing groups and newspapers) were masters at the inside game. While each casino likes to loudly argue for the public's right to spend their money however they see fit, that only really applies when they want permission to do

IF YOU'RE A STARTUP FACING
A DECISION WHETHER TO TRY TO MOBILIZE YOUR CUSTOMERS TO ADVOCATE FOR YOU POLITICALLY

 How much do your customers care about what you offer?

 How do your customers feel about going back to the status quo?

 Do you have enough customers to move the needle if mobilized?

 Do electeds care about your customers as voters?

 Can you turn your customer base into a political force?

something new like add more blackjack tables or slot machines. The rest of the time, they use their lobbyists and campaign donations to quietly try to kill any expansion of gaming that doesn't directly benefit them. But countering them in the halls of each statehouse was only how we'd avoid extinction, not how we'd win.

In a fight between longtime donors (the casinos) and two startups who were completely apolitical and ran lots of annoying ads on ESPN, the political firmament would always pick the donor. But just like Uber's rolling thunder, this was a case where Travis's Law could work.

Most people who play fantasy sports religiously are not politically active. Not only do most of them not know who their state rep is, half of them don't even know such a thing as a state rep even exists. Initially, that seemed like a disadvantage. Why would politicians care about people who never bother to vote?

But the more we thought about it, the more we realized the conventional wisdom might be wrong. Sure, most bros playing fantasy sports don't vote in local elections. But it's not just them—almost no one bothers to vote in most local elections (especially state legislative races). If we could credibly threaten to turn them into active voters, engaged and enraged by this one single issue, why would any politician stand in the way? This wasn't abortion. It wasn't same sex marriage or capital punishment. It was fantasy sports. Who cares? Why would anyone risk pissing off thousands of constituents over fantasy sports?

Collectively, FanDuel and DraftKings have 5 million customers in the United States (and Canada). That's the same size as either the NRA or Moveon.org. It's just a few million less than Planned Parenthood (8 million), bigger than SEIU (2 million), the Teamsters (1.5 million), and ten times the size of the ACLU (500,000).

Obviously, members and customers are not the same thing, but at least it gave us a base to work from. Matt, Seth London from our team, and I sat down and started going over the plan. (Seth had run grassroots efforts for both Obama campaigns, so his expertise was particularly useful.)

"Okay, where do we start? The usual Uber thing: Get them all tweeting and emailing their legislators?" I asked.

"I mean, sure, that's a start," Seth said. "But maybe we can take it in a new direction. Make our customers a genuine political movement."

"You think they care that much about this?"

"They fucking love fantasy sports."

"Okay, so what first? Half of them probably aren't even registered to vote."

"That's good," Matt said. "We register them and that alone sends a message. Say you're some state rep from central Florida. Not that many people vote in your usual election—probably around fifty thousand. All of a sudden, half that number registers to vote? That's terrifying in and of itself."

I nodded. "What else?"

"We make sure they know who's good and who's bad on our issue," Seth said. "They're on the app all the time. We already have their attention. We know what district they live in so even if they don't know who their state senator or state rep is, we do. We put their face smack on the app and brand them as good or bad for fantasy sports."

"I like that. We did a version of that for Ed Koch in 2010 when we ran this campaign to try to make Albany less corrupt."

"How'd that work out?" Matt laughed.

"Fair enough. But we created this pledge on issues like ethics reform and redistricting reform. If you signed it, we made you a hero of reform. If you didn't, you were an enemy. You even got a certificate. Pretty much everyone signed."

"Right," Seth said. "No politician wants to be branded as the bad guy."

"So we register them, we tell them who's with us and who's against us. Then what?"

"Then we mobilize them," Matt said. "What we've done with Uber. Use the app to connect them to their state senators and state reps. Email. Twitter. Facebook. When someone in state government hears from, like, fifty constituents, it's a tsunami. If we can generate even a few hundred . . ."

"It needs to be constant," I added. "We don't have to compete for their attention. We already have it. So let's not make it a onetime thing. Keep them informed. Keep them updated."

"And then we have to get out the vote," Seth said. "None of it matters if they're not ever going to take out their frustration in the next election. Door knocks. Phones. Social. Rides to the polls."

"Ubers to the polls," I jumped in.

We put it all in writing, went over it with Christian (who, luckily for us, saw the potential immediately), and got to work. By the end of that legislative session, we'd generated nearly half a million forms of direct contact to state legislators from over 150,000 customers (around 4 to 5 percent of the U.S. customer base). And once FanDuel got used to incorporating political messaging like "Let's get real, it's just fantasy," "Get your laws off my lineup," and "If only politics were skill-based" into its customer messaging, they got really good at it. Not every startup enjoys passionate customers willing to fight for you. But for those who do, fighting pay-to-play politics with real people is the single best weapon you have.

We ended up working on campaigns in more than thirty states, passing legislation in fifteen of them by the end of the 2017 legislative season. Some campaigns required a multifaceted attack including TV ads, lobbying, grassroots, polling, earned media, social media, and bringing in celebrities to wow lawmakers and help push our bill over the top (Tony Romo in Texas, Vinny Testaverde and Jim Kelly in New York). But what distinguished the effort to save fantasy sports from every other campaign of every advocacy group was the ability to make our voices heard not just through lobbying, not through campaign donations, but through real people—sometimes even real voters.

I wasn't expecting what came next, but the getting voters to the polls via Uber turned out to be a pretty useful idea to have in the back of my mind.

20

Riding the Sharing Economy to the Oval Office

Maggie Haberman knew about it before I did. (No surprise there.) "This Mike for President thing real?" she texted me.

"If it is, I'm not involved."

"If you're not involved, it ain't real."

Political reporters chase down rumors for a living, so I chalked Maggie's text up to that and went about my day. The next text told me it might be more than just a rumor. "You free this afternoon?" So far, emails, texts, and calls like that from Kevin Sheekey had led to my running Mike Bloomberg's 2009 mayoral campaign, working for Uber, and leading the charter school fight. So yes, I was free that afternoon.

Mike (mainly via Kevin) had looked at running for president in both 2008 and 2012 but didn't enter the race either time. He was already mayor during both of those elections, so letting them pass by didn't seem like as much of a missed opportunity. Now he was out of office, back at the helm as CEO of Bloomberg LP, and about to turn seventy-four. It was now or never.

On the one hand, Mike was a great candidate. Independent at a time when people distrusted both parties. Not a career politician. Made his money in technology, so it didn't engender the same hostility as people leaving hedge funds to run for office. Could self-finance, which meant he wouldn't owe anyone anything. Wouldn't have to hew to party orthodoxy on any issue.

On the other hand, he's not a natural politician. He's great at governing, but to Mike, running for office is the means to having the opportunity to govern. (For most politicians, the attention the campaign produces is the end, not the means.) Sparring every day with Hillary and Trump was not his idea of a good time. Despite having great credentials and essentially an unlimited amount of money, it's not clear the system was ready for an independent president. And since Mike was way too liberal to win a Republican primary and way too conservative to win a Democratic primary, running as what he actually was— not a member of any party—was the only option. In 1992, Ross Perot won around 20 percent of the popular vote and that was the high-water mark for an independent candidate. Beating that seemed doable, but winning 270 electoral college votes did not.

But what if we could prevent anyone from getting to 270? Then the race goes to the House of Representatives, and winning there didn't seem totally crazy. That was the biggest unknown in a series of many: whom would we actually be running against, was the public really ready for an independent, would Hillary survive the investigations into her email scandal, would Trump implode, and could we really win enough electoral votes to even send the race to the House?

If the race made it to the House, we'd pick up all of the Democratic-led delegations. (There weren't enough to put Hillary over the top, so in a choice between Mike and Trump, we'd get them.) But that meant we'd still need nine Republican states to vote for us. And since the House hadn't decided an election since Jefferson-Burr in 1800, none of the rules or laws around the process were clear (and to make matters worse, the Supreme Court, at the time, only had eight members).

I agreed to take a leave of absence from Tusk Holdings and run the campaign if Mike did pull the trigger. And that meant a successful launch was on my head. So we did what any Bloomberg-led project would do: We made a plan, did a lot of research, collected a lot of data, and put ourselves in position to launch in case Mike decided to run. That meant putting teams on the ground in states across the country so we could collect enough signatures to qualify for the ballot before each state deadline. Texas and North Carolina were first. We hired ballot access teams, local election counsel, and even rented offices in cities like San Antonio, Raleigh, and Houston. We conducted polling, focus groups, and started doing research into Trump. (My view was that Mike was the only candidate who'd have the credibility to attack Trump's business record and prove that Trump actually possesses little real-world business success.)

I told the team we had until the first week of March to decide and any later than that, I couldn't guarantee we'd have enough time to collect signatures and make the ballot in every state.

But those were just the basics. What excited me was the potential to use Mike's candidacy as a test case for all kinds of new ideas no one had ever tried before, both because we had plenty of money and because as an independent, we were tethered to fewer orthodoxies and restrictions than most candidates.

That February, I took a trip to San Francisco. I had the usual array of meetings with VCs and startups and tech reporters, but there was one group of meetings at the top of my list. The first was with Travis.

"If I'm willing to pay for a ride for every American to and from the polls on Election Day, would you put a Bloomberg button on the app?"

He thought about it for a moment. That could mean hundreds of millions in revenue on one day, and if any political candidate could actually afford it, it was Mike. It also could mean helping elect someone whom Travis—and most of Silicon Valley—venerated as a godfather of tech.

"Would that mean they have to vote for your guy?"

"This is America. They can vote for whoever they want. But if they're an Uber customer and they select the Bloomberg button, there's a pretty good chance they're with us. I already confirmed that you can do this with Trevor Potter, our election counsel. He used to run the Federal Election Commission."

"So he knows."

"He knows."

"I'm in."

"What if I want to offer campaign work to your drivers?"

"They're independent contractors. They can do whatever they want."

"But if I wanted a list of, say, drivers with a rating of 4.8 or higher in a dozen specific states, you could either give that to me or forward them an email?"

"Yep."

There was our grassroots team. Democrats can count on support—and bodies—from unions. Republicans can typically count on support—and bodies—from evangelicals. We weren't going to have either. And we didn't have an existing network of state and local party chapters to draw from. So we needed a supply of already-vetted independent contractors who could knock on doors, phone bank, hand out lit, and do all of the other work that comes with every campaign. Where can you find that? The sharing economy.

I then met with Ron Conway, a prolific and heavily connected venture capitalist in San Francisco. Ron was an early investor in Airbnb and a host of other sharing-economy companies. He didn't see why

Airbnb hosts couldn't choose to install Bloomberg yard signs or why DoorDash delivery people couldn't slip campaign literature under people's doors in between food runs.

While we didn't get the chance to execute the idea, I'm convinced it could materially increase turnout and activity for pro-technology, pro-innovation candidates. And while few candidates—if any—have the campaign budget of a Mike Bloomberg, the concepts above could be implemented on a smaller scale too.

You don't even need to be tech savvy to try the next idea. My view was that if we didn't do something that meaningfully distinguished Mike from the other candidates, we didn't stand a chance. One way to show a totally different approach and broaden our appeal to voters was by naming the entire cabinet during the campaign itself.

Mike's a master recruiter. If he spent most of his time convincing incredible people to join his cabinet, we could roll one out every week, and then say to the country, "One person doesn't run America. It takes a team of very talented people. If you like things the way they are, vote for one of the traditional candidates. But if you think this country is screwed up and needs to be fixed, America's best and brightest are here and willing to devote the next four years to solving our problems."

Had we done this, Mike obviously would have decided whom to recruit, but my initial list for consideration included people like Bill Gates (Secretary of State), Elon Musk (Energy), Oprah Winfrey (Commerce), Gabby Giffords (ATF), Ursula Burns (GSA), Warren Buffett (Treasury), Manny Diaz (HUD), Ray Kelly (FBI), Geoff Canada (Education), Reed Hastings (FCC), and Carl Pope (EPA).

Obviously, the idea came with risk. What if people said no? What if that leaked? What if it looked like we couldn't recruit the very best? Would our list be diverse enough to satisfy potential critics? What if we screwed up the vetting, proposed someone, and then the press found major skeletons in their closet?

But there was also no way to elect a nontraditional candidate without taking a lot of risk. A conventional campaign, I argued, would yield a conventional result—the third-party candidate loses. Recruiting and announcing the team before the election would highlight Mike's best attributes: management, recruiting, team building, demonstrating vision. It'd show he could work with a lot of different people, which is why you want an independent candidate. It'd also create a constant stream of content for reporters who need it at all times, and the endorsements from each person we'd announce would help fill the void from all of the endorsements a nontraditional presidential candidate wouldn't get (elected officials, unions, religious leaders, etc.).

As I concluded in my memo proposing the concept, "Even with the right opponents, a race that doesn't take risks, try new ideas, and shake things up is a race we didn't win. We have to take advantage of Mike's unique talents. We have to do things that are very different both substantively (ideas like this) and processwise (like co-opting the sharing economy as our field campaign), or the narrative of the campaign will be completely hijacked by Trump and we'll fail to get our message across. So while there are clear risks here, we can't afford not to be bold, not to be different, not to try."

In the end, neither idea mattered because Mike didn't run. We went back and forth on every issue, every permutation, every risk, and every outcome. Mike wanted to be president. He was willing to spend the money and put his reputation on the line. But not at the risk of electing Trump.

In our final meeting before he announced he wouldn't run, the discussion went something like this:

Mike: "So, Doug, how many states can we win outright?"
Doug: "With all the caveats of the unknown stipulated, around four or five."

Mike: "And that means what from an electoral college standpoint?"

Doug: "If that happened, it'd mean likely no one would get to 270 and the race would go to the House."

Mike, turning to the rest of us: "And in the House, how many states do we win?"

Me: "We should be solid for all of the Democratic states since the choice at that point would really be you versus Trump and not Hillary versus Trump, since there's no way Hillary could win any Republican-controlled delegations."

Mike: "So that's seventeen states, right?"

Me: "Right." Turned out it was a rhetorical question. (Mike's pretty good at math.)

Mike: "And the other nine?"

I then made my points about divided delegations, Paul Ryan, support from unusual GOP corners, running campaigns in GOP House districts to influence those members, etc. . . .

Mike: "So you're guaranteeing we get nine Republican states?"

Me: "Of course I can't guarantee that. I'm just giving you the plan for how we get there."

Mike: "And if it's eight?"

Me: "Trump wins."

Mike: "And if we don't run?"

Me: "Hillary wins." Everyone else around the table nodded in agreement.

Mike: "If I run, the chances of Trump winning go up. If I don't run, they don't. Issue settled."

In retrospect, Mike may have been the only thing standing between Trump and the White House. But we didn't know that at the time. I wish he had run, because the world would be a far safer and better place with Mike as president. And it would have been cool to be able to try out ideas like tapping into the sharing economy and announcing the full cabinet in advance. But even if Mike made the wrong decision, like always, he did it for the right reason.

I walked out of the room at the Bloomberg Foundation disappointed. The chance to run a presidential campaign with total freedom to innovate and an unlimited budget doesn't come around often (or ever, as it turns out). The chance to do it for someone I truly respected and admired made it a once-in-a-lifetime opportunity. So when the fact was that it was there for the taking, and then just went away, it wasn't easy to get over.

Back to politics as usual to protect our portfolio companies from the clutches of big, scared, old companies terrified of competition. And traditional politics turned out to be exactly what we needed to turn lemons into lemonade.

21

There's No One Way to Skin a Regulator

As I was trying to figure out how to run "Mike for President," Jordan Nof and the investment team were busy lining up more portfolio companies. A lot of venture capital revolves around trying to find a needle in the haystack. Most of the time, you end up covered in hay. But this time, Jordan found the needle.

If you gave a venture capitalist a lump of clay and asked him to mold the ideal startup founder, you'd get Daniel Schreiber. Imagine a CEO who has deep experience in tech on both the operations and marketing sides, has already founded a startup before, was an attorney, and has the balls of an Israeli, the savoir faire of a Brit, and the capitalist spirit of an American.

Daniel had recently founded Lemonade. I would have assumed insurance tech wouldn't be that interesting—and I would have assumed wrong. It's a great industry for startups. Insurance companies are massive, old, and stagnant, and incapable of innovating on their own, making them very ripe for disruption.

As the world's first peer-to-peer insurance company, Lemonade's concept was as simple as their model was radical: make the whole process of buying and using homeowners' or renters' insurance a lot cheaper and a lot easier. People buy homeowners' or renters' insurance. The money is put in a specific pool. Lemonade keeps 20 percent. The reinsurers (who basically make sure the insurance companies have the solvency needed to pay your home repair bills) keep 30 percent. And if the people in that specific pool don't use up the remaining money in claims, they get it back at the end of the year or can give it to a host of different charities. And because Lemonade was a fully and solely digital platform, when you don't have brokers, agents, offices, or Super Bowl ads, you can sell insurance for a lot less money.

Given the opportunity at hand to disrupt an industry as big as property and casualty insurance and given the company's outstanding leadership, Lemonade was an easy sell to VCs. Daniel and his brilliant cofounder Shai Wininger raised $26 million before they even had a product or an insurance license. But for the same reasons it was so attractive to investors, it was equally threatening to incumbent insurers, which wasn't a surprise. If you charge people twice as much, make your customers fill out endless paperwork just to sign up, and then fight them tooth and nail whenever they actually submit a claim, of course the concept of a startup like Lemonade threatens you. It should. What was surprising was how threatening the concept was to some regulators too.

The New York Department of Financial Services (DFS) is the bane of virtually every bank, insurance company, title company, cryptocurrency exchange, and anyone in the financial world who needs permission to operate in the state of New York. My friend Ben Lawsky created DFS with great ideas and good intentions, but when Ben left, the mentality of "let's be tough on everyone" remained—except without the same sophistication of when and how to apply it. Going after a bank that may have violated money laundering standards is different from bottling up a startup based in your own state that could save your own constituents thousands of dollars every year. Sometimes bureaucrats don't understand the power of their inaction. And sometimes they do, and exerting that power is what makes the job exciting to them.

Lemonade needed insurance licenses from every state, and given their New York headquarters and New York's status as the financial capital of the world, starting there made sense. Unfortunately, the bureaucrats at DFS had been giving them the runaround for months without really even any cogent explanation for why things were taking so long, so when Jordan spoke to Daniel, we had a receptive audience.

Jordan walked over to my desk. (We sit bullpen-style so everyone's just a few steps away.) "Can we get these guys an insurance license?"

Chris joined us, we asked a few questions, looked at each other, and I said, "I don't see why not. We're going to have to go over their heads. We're going to have to make this a political issue. And it's going to piss the people at DFS off. But if the choice is between angry bureaucrats or not being able to operate at all, you take the angry bureaucrats every time."

When Daniel heard how much equity we wanted to try to secure their insurance licenses in each state, he simply said, "This is either going to be the best deal I've ever done or the worst." We began immediately.

It only took a few calls with DFS to know that they weren't going to change their tune just because we were now involved. They didn't see their job as changing the system to fit new ideas and innovations. They saw their job as requiring new ideas to conform to their existing approaches, even if that meant nullifying all of the benefits of the new idea in the first place. To them, a new model for insurance meant a lot

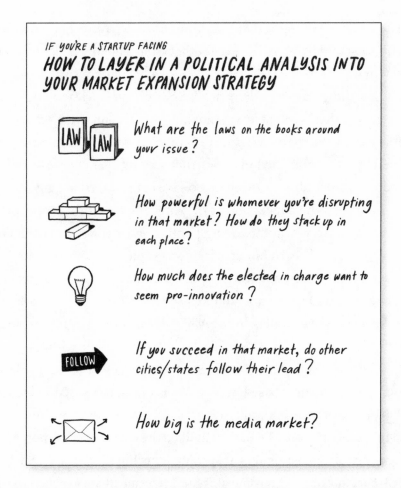

IF YOU'RE A STARTUP FACING

HOW TO LAYER IN A POLITICAL ANALYSIS INTO YOUR MARKET EXPANSION STRATEGY

What are the laws on the books around your issue?

How powerful is whomever you're disrupting in that market? How do they stack up in each place?

How much does the elected in charge want to seem pro-innovation?

If you succeed in that market, do other cities/states follow their lead?

How big is the media market?

of work—it meant that the beliefs and practices they'd built up over years and years might no longer be applicable. And being told by some startup that they needed to move a lot faster was reason enough to strangle them in the crib. DFS tells companies what to do. Not the other way around.

Talking with the regulators wasn't going to suffice. We took an inventory of our options and the path was clear: We needed the governor's office to overrule DFS and we knew the governor's office would only do that if the political cost of not approving Lemonade was more than they wanted to bear. Keep in mind, regulators typically aren't elected. They're appointed. Making the taxpayers happy is not their problem. Their bosses, on the other hand, run for reelection every few years.

What did going over their heads mean? Our nuclear option was announcing that Lemonade was moving their headquarters out of New York because the state was so anti-innovation, so bureaucratic, so corrupted by the entrenched interests that staying there was untenable. London was already recruiting Lemonade to relocate there anyway, so our threat had the added benefit of being true. And for New York's governor, Andrew Cuomo, being publicly embarrassed over the intransigence of his own bureaucracy was even worse than the actual impact of losing Lemonade's jobs and presence. In this case, we had honey and vinegar to deploy, and we used them both.

We hired Mike Avella, one of Albany's top lobbyists, to start making the case to the governor's office. We started meeting with friends at other state agencies who saw the value in a new, low-cost, highly differentiated insurer based in New York. (The state's Economic Development Corporation wanted Lemonade's jobs to stay in New York and the state's Housing Department liked the idea of easy-to-purchase, easy-to-use, low-cost renters' insurance entering the marketplace.)

But we also mixed in some vinegar. Menashe Shapiro, who ran our research shop, started compiling a list of campaign donations to Governor Cuomo by the insurance industry. The comms team started preparing pitches about pay-to-play politics and regulatory capture. We prepared a letter from a host of major VCs to the governor saying that if New York couldn't license a company like Lemonade, there was no reason to invest in New York's tech sector. We created an online petition calling on the governor to respect consumer rights.

Then we started bringing in legislators to call DFS and the governor's office to make the case. We made enough progress for the

IF YOU'RE A STARTUP FACING
AN ATTACK FROM AN ENTRENCHED
INTEREST YOU'RE DISRUPTING

 What's the public perception:
Sympathetic or sleazy?

 Are they politically influential:
Political power & campaign donations?

 How ethical are they?

 How important are they to the elected
official's policy goals?

 Do they have powerful allies?

governor's office to ask DFS about it, but at first that only got the regulators' backs up even more. (How dare we go over their heads!) But as we kept the pressure on, DFS started changing their tune. And the political people at the top of the agency started getting nervous. We were making headway, but not fast enough to meet Daniel's goal of launching by June.

Eventually, I got frustrated, called Avella, and said, "Tell the governor's office that they have a choice. Tomorrow's *Wall Street Journal* can say that New York just approved a new startup to start providing low-cost insurance to consumers. Or it can say that one of the hottest startups around just left New York because the governor and his team prefer bureaucracy to jobs." Avella probably relayed the message a lot more politely, and it still didn't get done within twenty-four hours, but a few days later, we got the notification. Lemonade was approved. There was some paperwork to fill out, but the decision had been made.

We then proceeded to seek insurance licenses in the rest of the country. Every state was different. California was slow but reasonable. (It doesn't hurt that the insurance commissioner in California is independently elected, so the prospect of providing his constituents with new, low-cost, easy-to-use insurance offered appeal.)

We needed legislation in Florida to reduce the surplus capital requirement for insurers. Florida deliberately has an extremely condensed legislative session (around two months) to reinforce the notion that good government means less government. Passing a new law just to help one insurance startup seemed highly unlikely. But the combination of the right inside game (our lobbyist, Brian Ballard, is the best there is in Florida and knew exactly when to strike) and an overwhelming outside game (we mobilized tons of fans and bombarded the legislature) was enough to get it done.

Texas, true to their "open for business" reputation, welcomed us to the state and gave us a license almost the minute we asked for one. Illinois was surprisingly easy too. Pennsylvania was more of a pain than it needed to be. But the validation from New York was ultimately enough for everyone else, and by the middle of the next year, Lemonade had the credibility and paperwork to make their case nationwide. Soon after, Lemonade began setting records for selling new insurance policies faster than any company in history. (The fact that they pay out claims in as little as three seconds doesn't hurt.) For the same reasons that disrupting the insurance industry wasn't all that complicated, running roughshod over them politically wasn't that complicated either.

A DECISION WHETHER TO TAKE ON A POLITICAL FIGHT IN ANY GIVEN JURISDICTION

 What tools do you have at your disposal?

 Do you have the moral high ground?

 How interested is the press in your issue?

 How much money can you dedicate to this fight?

 Do you have other politically valuable assets? (Jobs, tax revenue)

 Can you make this a consumer rights issue?

 Are there other political dynamics at play? (understand the political landscape)

Daniel, Shai, and their team understood that every situation was different, every jurisdiction was different, and that allowing us to use all of the tools in our arsenal would get them what they needed. But Lemonade is also a lot more sophisticated than most startups, many of whose founders and CEOs either think that the rightness of their argument, the genius of their platform, or the value of their product should be enough to get any regulator to see things their way. It's not.

Ultimately, regulators report to politicians. And politicians are far more likely to do what you want if you can either imperil their chances of keeping their job or help them achieve their political goals (staying in office or winning the next office).

The good news is, startups have a lot more tools at their disposal than most realize: a good narrative that gets the media interested, a strong inside game, money for ads, the ability to threaten to leave town, the moral high ground to accuse the other side of pay-to-play, and the ability to label the politician at hand either protech or antitech.

In other words, there are a lot of ways to skin a cat. Knowing what's in your arsenal, how to use it, and when to use it is what matters most. But if we thought insurance was complicated, we soon learned how easy it was compared to a genuinely controversial topic: cannabis.

22

Uber for Weed

don't support the War on Drugs. Hundreds of thousands of Americans are sent to jail every year unnecessarily for nonviolent drug offenses. Tens of billions of dollars of taxpayer money every year are wasted arresting, prosecuting, and imprisoning nonviolent drug offenders. Keeping drugs illegal enables cartels in Latin America to flourish and gangs in the United States to proliferate, causing endless amounts of senseless deaths and violence for no good reason whatsoever. Alcohol is often just as dangerous as most illegal drugs, and while alcoholism is a problem, once we ended Prohibition in 1933, the purchase of alcohol at least no longer came with gangs, violence, black-market trading, and smuggling. Alcohol today is taxed, regulated, and controlled. Drugs should be treated the same way. I believe drugs should be decriminalized.

That's why I was eager to work in cannabis tech—it was one of the rare issues that had massive economic upside and aligned perfectly with my own views. Our work in the sector began with Eaze, which is known as Uber for weed. Eaze was founded by Keith McCarty, who had startup experience as an early employee of Yammer, a social networking service that was quickly acquired by Microsoft for more than $1 billion in cash.

The concept was simple: it was like ordering pizza or sushi online, except they could also connect you, via telemedicine, to a doctor to prescribe a Cannabis Card if you needed one. And once you had a card, they'd connect you to a dispensary who would take your order and bring it to you. Where cannabis was legal (either medicinally or recreationally), there was no reason why consumers shouldn't be able to order it just like they do any other product. But this wasn't any other product. In California, each city was empowered to set its own rules around cannabis delivery, so the politics of weed were hazy at best.

Seth Webb started working on Eaze and quickly developed a to-do list: make delivery legal in key California markets with long-standing bans like Los Angeles, San Jose, and Anaheim; overturn recent bans in cities like Freemont, Irvine, and Torrance; and kill bans under consideration in cities like Sacramento and Long Beach. Like any political issue, we started figuring out what narrative would work and whom we could count on to support us.

In states where cannabis is legal recreationally, the argument is around consumer rights. But in California, where (at the time), only medicinal use was permitted, we had an even better constituency: people who needed marijuana to treat their cancer, epilepsy, and a host of other diseases.

Seth started meeting with local residents in each city who used cannabis to alleviate their medical problems and we started telling their stories to reporters, especially in San Jose, where we felt like the local powers that be were open enough to the idea that a quick win was feasible.*

The San Jose city council had already banned cannabis delivery— twice. But still, they weren't completely hostile to the idea. They were facing the same internal struggle that politicians often face when they know an issue's time has come but their incredible aversion to doing *anything* that could risk their next election still gave them pause. California had offered legal medicinal marijuana for years. Reefer Madness was a parody at this point, not a real-world concern. Just Say No, in California, applied far more to coal-fired power plants, gas-guzzling cars, GMO-modified foods, and wearing suits and ties than it did to vilifying cannabis. The local pols knew it was time. They just needed a push.

We launched an inside game fight to work on the mayor, city attorney, police department, fire department, planning and zoning departments, and the city council to argue for and then develop a delivery policy. We had to demonstrate that the status quo had given rise to dozens of illegal operators the police couldn't control and show how unregulated delivery both threatened community safety and deprived the city of valuable tax dollars. We had to present Eaze as the proven, safe, and secure alternative, and encourage the council to develop new rules to ensure Eaze's operation. We needed six votes on the city council (out of eleven) and felt like we had three potential supporters and two clear opponents—the rest were up for grabs.

---

* I was joking around with Seth one day about Eaze. Unlike all of our other startups, we didn't have to worry about political payback from the people Eaze was disrupting—the drug cartels. "They can kill us," we joked, "but they can't lobby against us." And then I thought, It'd be pretty funny if they could. That led to Honest Work, a TV pilot I wrote about a campaign to legalize recreational cannabis in Illinois with the venture capitalists running the Yes campaign and the drug cartels running the No campaign.

So we launched an outside game—mobilizing the sixteen legal medical-marijuana collectives in San Jose and an initial grassroots universe of ten thousand patients to make the case publicly. We needed to tell their stories properly and widely, which led to an online patient petition, patient testimonials shared with lawmakers, and a short animated video explaining how Eaze works, why a delivery ban hurts patients, and what San Jose residents could do to help overturn the ban.

We unleashed a constant barrage of tactics hitting the council every day that summer while working behind the scenes with the city manager's office. Our polling showed that 69 percent of registered voters supported allowing delivery, and eventually, we won the favor of the city hall staff and wore the council down, winning a vote that October to legalize delivery by capturing eight out of eleven possible votes.

We won because we embraced the need for new regulation, embraced the need to engage politically, spent time and money, worked hard, assembled a coalition, mobilized our supporters, developed the right narrative, and conveyed the right message. In other words, we won because Eaze was willing to be proactive and dedicate time and resources to the fight.

And while San Jose's legalization both opened up a big market for Eaze (it's the third-biggest city in California and the tenth-biggest in the United States) and gave Eaze a precedent to use in other markets, it's still a city-by-city, ordinance-by-ordinance fight. Los Angeles's legalization became possible through an L.A. County referendum the next spring, and sooner or later, each market will permit delivery, first in California and one day, everywhere.

But that day may not come for a while. While some states permit cannabis use, federal law does not. Cannabis is considered a Schedule I drug by the DEA, just like heroin or cocaine. That's why there are no real banking services for cannabis businesses. (Banks are too afraid the feds might take their money.) The same applies to interstate commerce and advertising. Until cannabis is moved to Schedule II, there will always be a lot of regulatory uncertainty in the market, no matter how many local campaigns we manage to win.

And the more regulatory uncertainty there is, the more most VC funds can't participate in cannabis deals. (Their investors won't allow it.) That means cannabis tech companies can't afford to do what most startups do—lose money while building a product and a customer base. That creates a vicious cycle that makes it hard for any cannabis tech company to really succeed until the federal laws are changed, which will not happen during the Trump presidency. (Trump is too wedded to his very conservative base to change course on this issue—the politics for Trump are very different than they were for the San Jose city council.)

So in this case, while we won the battle of San Jose, as long as the federal rules remain stagnant, we're likely to lose the war. At best, the market won't really open up until late 2021 (and realistically, sometime in 2022). That was a lesson I at least already understood. The next fight taught me a lesson that had never occurred to me before: Sometimes people choose to lose important battles simply because the cost of winning is even higher.

23

Protecting the Brand
May Mean Losing the Fight

Taking down regulators and entrenched interests works if you have so much riding on the outcome, you're willing to fight to the death to get what you need. Lemonade was willing because they couldn't operate without insurance licenses. FanDuel was willing because the alternative was to be banned in states across the country. Everyone knows Uber was willing. Tesla wasn't.

Still, it was kind of cool to get a cold email from Sam Teller, Elon Musk's chief of staff. Tesla needed someone to run politics and government relations and Sam wanted to know if I'd be interested. I was having way too much fun creating Tusk Ventures to consider it, but it would have been professional malpractice to not at least pitch them on hiring us to do the work as a consultant.

Sam and I met on his next trip to New York. He was as impressive as you'd expect for someone keeping the trains running for Elon and his multiple worlds (Tesla, SolarCity, SpaceX, The Boring Company, Hyperloop One). I think he was hoping to convince me to consider the job and I was hoping to convince him to hire us to solve Tesla's political problems (mainly that most state auto-dealer laws prohibit Tesla from selling direct to consumers), so we both agreed it'd make sense for me to fly to San Francisco and meet with Elon.

A friend of mine whose wife worked for Tesla sent me a link to a 350-page blog post on "Wait but Why?" about Elon, whom they called "the world's raddest man." Six hours and three thousand miles later, I was both excited and a little scared to meet him. Even though he's around a million times smarter than me, I knew that when we got to talking about politics, I'd be just fine. But reports in the blog post (and other articles) about meetings with Elon were a little disconcerting—he may not face you, he may not say anything the entire time, he may ask you questions you clearly have no idea how to answer, and so on.

None of that happened. He couldn't have been more normal— calm, engaged, focused, on topic. We met for forty-five minutes and I outlined both why I couldn't come work for him and why he needed us to fight the auto dealers in each state. Tesla had taken on some of these fights already, winning some battles and losing others.

"Look," I said, "car dealers are a tough opponent. They're the one local mainstay in every assembly district, every state senate district. It's like *Friday Night Lights*—Buddy was the most influential guy in town and he owns the local car dealerships. They sponsor the little league teams. Give out candy on Halloween. And donate reliably to every local and state politician every single election."

He nodded. "Keep going."

"You guys bring a lot of star power to any political fight. Tesla's a very cool brand. You're a celebrity. That's enough to put you guys in the game. But there's a reason they say all politics are local. And your brand is literally about moving people to Mars, not mobilizing voters in state representative primaries."

"So what do we need to do?"

"Go hard at these fuckers. Show they're using money to keep the legislators in line—and in doing that, they're taking away all of the jobs you could create in each state and they're also forcing everyone to breathe dirty air."

He nodded again. It seemed like he was on board with the strategy. We signed a contract with Tesla a few days later and got to work.

It was clear to us that taking a conventional approach to passing legislation to allow Tesla to open stores to sell cars directly to consumers (rather than forcing them to go through auto dealers and pay a steep markup) would yield a conventional result: failure. Just announcing the idea, rounding up a few legislators to sponsor the bill, and then trying to push the bill through committee, each chamber, and the entire legislative process may be the normal course of action for most lobbyists and most campaigns, but Tesla's opponent was too tough to overcome with the usual behavior. Tesla gave us their list of priority states—Connecticut, Indiana, Michigan, Texas, New York. We came back with a list of tactics, none of them gentle.

- **Connecticut:** Opposition research into every state senator to see where they're vulnerable. Whom are they taking money from? Where are they hypocritical? (For example, Tesla's main opponent in the senate claimed to be an environmentalist but consistently took anticlimate votes on energy bills.) Robo calls into every district urging constituents to call their senators to support our bill with specific negative connotations in the call about every senator against us.

IF YOU'RE A STARTUP FACING
AN ATTACK FROM A POLITICIAN WHO TAKES MONEY FROM WHOMEVER YOU'RE DISRUPTING

 What's driving his/her decision? Politics or policy?

 Can you turn his/her narrative against them?

 What type of coalition of supporters can you build?

 Can you devote real resources to the fight? (money, ads, events, PR, resources, and expertise)

 Can you mobilize your customers to weigh in on your behalf?

- **Indiana:** Go after General Motors hard. GM was behind many of the anti-Tesla bills around the country. (If anyone symbolized an old, broken, entrenched interest it was GM and if anyone symbolized a new, innovative startup, it was Tesla.) GM, we felt, could be attacked on their unholy alliance with the United Auto-workers (which would play well in a Republican state like Indiana) and on their failure to clean up brownfields (which would play well with Democrats). While GM wasn't the scourge of

Hoosiers everywhere, they were a better target than the local, often beloved auto dealers.

- **Michigan:** Robo calls in every district to spur fear among legislators and prompt outreach by their constituents. A new website designed solely to attack the speaker of the House and the State Republican party for pay-to-play politics and corruption. Threaten to call for investigations into the speaker's ethics to get his staff worried enough to stop opposing us and start negotiating.

- **Texas:** Go hard on the economic-freedom/conservative/libertarian angle: direct mail, grassroots outreach, maybe even TV ads. People shouldn't have to go to an auto dealer and pay more money just to buy a car. Government shouldn't decide how cars are sold or how people should be allowed to buy them. This is an issue for the free market, not intrusive government regulation. Engage conservative talk radio and conservative policy groups to spread the word.

- **New York:** Go after pay-to-play politics by pointing out the donations each local politician had taken from the auto dealers and accusing them of keeping Tesla out of the market because that's exactly what they'd been paid to do by their donors. Add in calling out the state's shoddy economy (outside of New York City) to show that any efforts to limit new jobs meant that all of the political rhetoric about reviving and rebuilding the upstate economy was bullshit.

Every morning at 7 a.m., either Menashe Shapiro or Haley Rubinson from our team would send out the daily email listing all of the opportunities, tactics, and plans for each state. Every day, we'd push and argue for permission to start actually doing these things. But we kept getting stuck.

"These are rough topics," a typical conversation would start.

"Yes, that's the point," we'd answer.

"They're going to make people mad."

"That's also the point."

"We're a company that makes people excited, inspired, happy."

"In your marketing of cars, sure. But the 'Hey, we're Tesla, you should love us' shtick isn't going to work in most state legislatures."

"But if we do these things, we could be criticized."

"Not could. You will be criticized. No one likes being attacked. No one likes being called corrupt or hypocritical. They're going to attack back."

"But our brand."

"What about it?"

"Attack websites. Nasty phone calls. Opposition research. Accusations. None of that is how we want Tesla to be seen. And it's not how Elon would want to be positioned."

"Don't you want to be able to sell cars in these states?"

"Of course we do."

"And has the normal approach worked in any of them so far?"

"No."

"So this is what it takes."

"We'll get back to you."

Then we'd repeat the cycle again a few days later. Everyone we dealt with at Tesla was very smart—it's not like they didn't understand that if they wanted to win, they'd have to take some risks and absorb some blows. But Tesla's brand, its image, its reputation, and, perhaps most important, its share price depended on maintaining a patina of positive social change. What we were proposing was a pupu platter of some of the nastiest tactics politics had to offer.

I don't know if the government relations team was getting direction

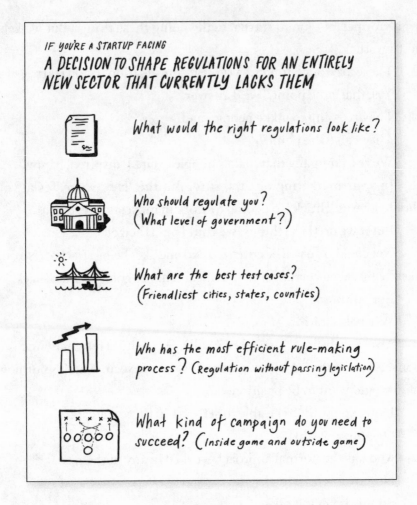

IF YOU'RE A STARTUP FACING

A DECISION TO SHAPE REGULATIONS FOR AN ENTIRELY NEW SECTOR THAT CURRENTLY LACKS THEM

What would the right regulations look like?

Who should regulate you?
(What level of government?)

What are the best test cases?
(Friendliest cities, states, counties)

Who has the most efficient rule-making process? (Regulation without passing legislation)

What kind of campaign do you need to succeed? (Inside game and outside game)

from above or just applying what they'd been told on other issues to our stuff. There were allusions to calls with Elon to make our case on being tough but the calls never happened. So instead, we went through the 2016 legislative sessions fighting the traditional fight. Our lobbyists asked members to support the bill because it was the right thing to do. They made the usual arguments for job creation and clean air in the usual ways. They ran into the buzzsaw of the auto dealer's popularity and entrenched relationships in each community and each district. And we lost, time and time again.

Was Tesla wrong to prioritize their brand over their politics? Maybe not. What do I know? I've never created a $50 billion–plus company. It's easy to see how protecting the brand at all costs became their internal mantra. But it's hard to see how avoiding all political risk would lead to new laws over the objections of people who'd been playing the game a lot longer and a lot better than Tesla ever had.

This is a real problem for startups and tech companies in general. The positive media attention, the customer adoration, and the high valuations or market caps are all extremely dependent on their image as innovative, new, positive forces for change. Positive forces for change usually don't run scorched-earth political campaigns. Positive forces for change also usually don't accomplish much politically because without the pain that comes with making politicians think they may lose their seat if they don't work with you, they usually just don't work with you at all.

Tesla seems to be winning the war. But in our case, being unwilling to do what it took to change the dynamic of each campaign in each state meant they lost each battle, each time.

24

Always Carry Enough Cash

t's gonna be huge," the tech evangelists on my team argued.

"It's never going to work," the people who had worked in government and politics argued back.

I should have trusted Bob Greenlee and his team. They understood regulation. They understood politics. The people recommending My-Table to me understood neither. But I liked the concept and the success we were having was getting to my head, so I agreed—wrongly—to take them on.

MyTable was an L.A.-based startup that took the same concept that has made Uber and Airbnb so successful and tried to apply it to your kitchen. Just like people use their Toyota to make extra money by giving other people rides and people use their couch to make extra money by letting people pay to sleep on it, in this case, people would cook, post their offerings on the MyTable platform, and other people could buy it. Imagine you live alone and you love lasagna. You can't really make one serving of lasagna—you have to make a tray. To help cover the cost of the ingredients and your time, you can post, say, half the lasagna on the platform and sell it to someone else. (They can pick it up or have it delivered.) MyTable's business model was no different from Airbnb's or any online marketplace—take a piece of the transaction each and every time.

On the one hand, this made sense. Why shouldn't people be able to monetize their kitchen? And while the idea of buying food from a stranger's kitchen may seem crazy, how well do you know 99 percent of the restaurants you order from on Seamless? And is buying lasagna from a stranger that much weirder than getting in their car or sleeping on their couch? Platform businesses are attractive because you're just connecting buyers and sellers, so the technology is fairly simple and the execution lies mainly in attracting people on both sides of the equation to the platform.

On the other hand, it made absolutely no sense. Departments of Health in every city, everywhere, inspect commercial kitchens. They make sure that food being sold to the public isn't poisoned, isn't contaminated, and isn't made in a kitchen overrun by rodents. And while many government regulations are either the product of someone else just trying to stifle competition or a politician wanting attention, protecting public health and safety is probably the most legitimate reason for government to exist.

There's no way health inspectors can start showing up in the kitchen of everyone who wants to sell their leftover lasagna to make sure the conditions are acceptable. I understood this going in, but thought we could develop a self-regulatory system to appease regulators: people would order their ingredients from a centralized, inspected location, we could livestream the preparation and cooking, we could have each seller sign an affidavit affirming they met a set of standards, and we could have a strict reporting system where any issues are quickly investigated by the platform. It was a major departure from the way things were currently done, but that's the whole point of disruption.

MyTable was run by a smart, competent CEO named James Jerlecki, who understood that solving the inspection riddle was essential. James had managed to convince his six investors that the problem was solvable, and given how much some of my own employees loved the concept, it's not hard to see how investors who weren't that steeped in politics and regulation could look past the regulatory risk.

Not shockingly, soon after launching, MyTable was shut down by the health department in Austin, and then again in Los Angeles. We expected that. We made a list of cities that had tech-friendly mayors (and where we had good relationships; we did the same with states and tech-friendly governors) with the idea of piloting a self-regulatory framework there first, proving it worked, and using that to expand to other markets.

We began with Providence and started talking to the city and the state. (There was some overlapping jurisdiction and Governor Gina Raimondo has a venture capital background, so if any politician understood the concept of looking at regulations differently to accommodate new technologies, she did.) The challenge was that governments move slowly, and absent a jurisdiction agreeing to a framework with us, MyTable couldn't operate and they couldn't make money. James was running through his funding to keep the lights on, which meant he had limited time for something to happen. He couldn't afford lobbyists, which we desperately needed to push the idea in multiple jurisdictions at the same time. There were a few other startups in the same space trying the same concept—Josephine, Umi Kitchen—but none of them wanted to work together, so we couldn't even pool everyone's resources. (Not every industry association works, but a number of our portfolio companies like FanDuel, Handy, and even Uber at times have

been able to work with competitors to solve common regulatory problems even while still trying to kill each other in every other way.)*

Supporting a team of a dozen people is expensive (especially when
you only raise under $2 million to begin with) and James ran out of
money in about six months, long before we could get health officials in
Providence to come around to a radically different approach to inspection and regulation. Without much fanfare, MyTable went bankrupt
and we learned a valuable lesson—it's fine to take on uphill battles, but
if the resources to fight aren't there, winning is unlikely. I should have
known that going in.

---

* With that said, if you're fighting an existential battle, you're usually better off going it alone.
Dying because you fought hard and lost is one thing. Dying because no one in your coalition
could agree on a strategy or make a decision is a lot worse. Yes, there are times where the only way
to afford a real campaign is to join forces—and that's what the food-sharing sector should have
done. But that's still, to me, more the exception than the rule.

25

Who Needs the *Today* Show?

They're a service, a delivery mechanism. We're not promising to help people lose weight or grow back their hair." Michaela Balderson from our comms team was yelling loud enough into her phone that the whole bullpen heard it.

She kept going. "You guys are missing the point—Care/of is like Harry's or Warby Parker. Not GNC or the Vitamin Shoppe. In fact, Care/of's entire existence is the polar opposite of those dinosaurs—it's to give consumers honest, transparent information around vitamins."

We all heard a few "ughs" and "you're still missing the points" and then the phone slammed hard into the receiver.

Featuring one of our fastest-growing portfolio companies on the *Today* show would have been a coup—lots of exposure to a new audience, and lots of credibility bestowed by the *Today* show's (at the time) sterling reputation.

But when a startup launches in an industry specifically to both exploit and fix all of the problems caused by the incumbents in its field, in some ways, it also inherits the bad karma of the industry they're trying to change.

In this case, the *Today* show wanted to profile Care/of—a new, online vitamin and supplement startup that curates your daily intake and sends you a box each month with each day's vitamins in its own pouch—as one of the "best new subscription services to sign up for." But the producers and the lawyers saw the segment very differently.

Dr. Mehmet Oz had run into controversy over promoting miracle weight-loss products that had no scientific basis or backing. And since Dr. Oz made these claims on his syndicated TV show, once the issue reached enough of a frenzy to force him to appear before a U.S. Senate subcommittee to answer for these dubious claims (and, more important, to leverage his celebrity to get attention for the senators demanding answers), NBC was freaked out about promoting any type of vitamin or supplement. It didn't matter that Care/of was an online service and had no interest in making any health claims on the show, or that the producers loved it and used the product themselves. All that mattered was the lawyers for the *Today* show—much like regulators—didn't fully grasp what the company did. Worried about another controversy, they spiked the segment. (Given what we now know about the *Today* show, it seems pretty clear their lawyers were focusing on the wrong things.) Michaela's final mutterings of frustration made it clear the *Today* show segment was dead, but there was a lot more we could do.

When I first heard that Americans spend $39 billion every year on vitamins and supplements, I was floored. Spending $39 billion on gasoline or milk and bread didn't sound crazy. But vitamins? Especially in an industry that wasn't dominated by any one brand and was led by

behemoth chains like GNC and the Vitamin Shoppe, where typically
the guy behind the counter just told you whatever he needed to to make
a sale as quickly as possible and get his commission.

That's why Patrick Chun and Jed Cairo decided to make a vitamin and supplement company their first foray out of Juxtapose, a
Manhattan-based incubator that conceives and launches one new
startup each year to massively disrupt an entrenched industry. Jordan
knew Patrick from his Blackstone days and since Juxtapose's model
(raising money to spend most of their time thinking and then to build
just one company every twelve months) was as weird and unconven-
tional as ours (getting into deals by leveraging politics), naturally we all
started working together.

When we first met with Jed and Patrick about Care/of, it didn't
take long to understand the value proposition—make choosing, buying, and taking vitamins easier and less confusing for consumers.
We'd talked to a few other startups in the space before, but they all
wanted us just to tell them how they could make all kinds of specious
health claims without getting in trouble. We don't mind using our
powers to beat the crap out of people, but we usually do it to help new
startups compete, innovate, and offer something better to consumers.
That often means changing the laws or defying regulators, but not for
the purpose of just doing what the entrenched interests in that field are
already doing in the first place.

Care/of was different. They wanted the exact opposite—guidance
on what laws to comply with; making sure they didn't claim anything
that wasn't completely permissible, supportable, and legit; and making
sure they were more focused on building the product and service delivery than just promoting themselves and the brand. In other words, they
were a completely responsible startup, defying the stereotypes at almost every turn. With Michaela's help, Craig Ebert and his team built
a new model to market the company.

In the old days, if you wanted to promote a vitamin or supplement, you'd go to the producer of a soft news show (just like we did with the *Today* show), give them a sample, pressure them to promote the product on the show, and then hope the people watching at home would go to the store to buy the product or maybe order it online.

The *Today* show didn't work out. But that may have been a blessing in disguise. Instead, Craig, Michaela, and the team recruited social media health and wellness and beauty influencers like Hannah Bronfman and Into The Gloss, each with hundreds of thousands of followers, and worked with them to post reviews of the product, pictures, and commentary on their channels—Instagram, Snapchat, and Facebook.

Influencers are the new editors. Long gone are the days where you pitch editors at big-name magazines like *Vogue* or *Elle*. You're far better off working with the people on Instagram and Twitter who have the most followers—people who began by organically and independently blogging about fashion or health or video games and just kept getting more and more attention. But far more important, they gained people's trust.

Let's say we had gotten that *Today* show segment. Do viewers trust Savannah Guthrie? Some do, but she's implicitly promoting an array of ideas, products, and services on every single show. That makes the value of her endorsement of any one product pretty limited. Heavily followed influencers on social media are not only more credible and more persuasive, but you can then buy the products they like on the very same platform with just a few swipes. That's a far more efficient way to reach customers and sell product. And while product influencers haven't been brought in yet to help startups fight off bad politics, it's only a matter of time.

Then the team went a step further. Every Care/of box has thirty or thirty-one (depending on the month) individual packages. They made each individual packet "Instagram-worthy" with creative aesthetics and personalized messages (like, "Hi, Bradley, how's it going?"), quizzes, and different designs. They knew the better the packaging, the more likely their (often millennial) customers would be to post photos of each packet, spurring a larger following and more customers.

We also used all of the traditional media channels to promote Care/of—including the holy grail of tech publications like Recode, TechCrunch, VentureBeat, and *Forbes,* but that was more to generate familiarity and validation within the Valley than to acquire actual consumers. The tech press cared about the usual metrics: how much money Care/of raised, how many customers they had, their customer acquisition costs, and their growth plans. Those are all important topics for the tech community, but none of them matter to people buying vitamins. In the world of social media, all press is different.

Some press is useful in reaching specific people you need (investors, partners, vendors). Some press is useful in forcing politicians and regulators to deviate from the normal course of business (taking care of their donors and other special interests until someone calls them out on it loudly enough). Some press is useful in reaching consumers and potential customers. (Although the power of social media is quickly eclipsing the power of earned media, and in a perfect campaign, you're using both in tandem.)

Knowing which to employ, when, is critical. But even more important, being willing to deviate from the norms goes a long way. Sometimes, like Tesla, deviating from the norms means being tougher and nastier than you'd prefer. (So much so that Tesla chose not to do it, preferring to lose a legislative fight than risk their overall reputation.) And sometimes, like Care/of, it means embracing regulation, recognizing that the traditional approaches don't necessarily work, and trying new things. Not every intersection of tech and politics has to be a fight.*

Like everything at the nexus of politics and tech, it's all about context. But working with startups who can think creatively and ethically at the same time goes a long way.

---

* To help facilitate more cooperation and less strife, we've been working with the Rockefeller Foundation's 100 Resilient Cities initiative to bring cities, venture capitalists, and startups together to discuss ways that new technologies and ideas can solve long-term problems like traffic and wastewater disposal—problems that have vexed many cities for decades. It's still early but so far, so good—everyone involved on both ends (tech and cities) has been excited about not just the potential to implement new ideas but also the chance to work together instead of against one another.

SECTION V

Where Do We Go from Here?

26

The Biggest Disruption Fight of Them All

Every founder and entrepreneur reading this is probably wondering, "Isn't there a technological solution to politics as we know it?" As a matter of fact, there is.

If you ask most people what's the biggest problem facing our democracy, once they finish venting about waste and corruption, they'll tell you that government is too polarized, too dysfunctional, and nothing gets done. On that count, they're right. But they assume—incorrectly—that it's because people in office are dumb and lazy. On that count, they're wrong.

The vast, vast majority of elected officials are highly logical around their underlying goal: winning office and staying in office. They know who actually bothers to vote, and they tailor their views, votes, policies, and actions almost exclusively to cater to the people who can elect or unelect them. And given that those who vote (especially in primaries at all levels of government) tend to be highly partisan and highly ideological, the people they elect then religiously represent their views. That means little gets done, and when something does get done, it's because one party has captured a legislative body or executive office and their actions are usually pretty extreme.

The problems we face—climate change, crime and violence, not enough good jobs, income inequality, bad schools, expensive health care, racial strife—are far too big and far too difficult to solve when every political signal to an elected official represents the views of the few at the expense of the many.

As we've seen in the fights for Uber, Handy, FanDuel, Lemonade, Tesla, Care/of, Eaze, and so on, if you know how to frame your issue—both politically and publicly—you can usually reach the right outcome. But imagine a world where you didn't have to do that in the first place—a world where the best interests of politicians and the best interests of the public were actually aligned.

It's possible because most politicians are highly adaptable. If 15 percent of their constituents vote in their primary, they'll represent the views of those 15 percent. If 85 percent vote, they'll represent their views. So the more people vote, the more mainstream our politicians become. And when politicians are all acting within the mainstream, that allows them to—finally—work together and get things done.

This all depends upon the mainstream actually bothering to vote. We know most people don't bother when the only choice is going to a polling place. Would mobile voting change that?

The skeptics say, "No. Millennials are apathetic. They won't vote no matter how easy you make it. And most other people won't either."

The work we've done over the past five years mobilizing grassroots political advocacy for companies like FanDuel and Uber shows otherwise. Because we're able to reach people while they're already on their phones using the Uber or FanDuel platforms, we can easily explain the issue to them, lay out the stakes, and with the push of a button, they can express their views to the relevant elected official. And they've done it—repeatedly, all over the country. As a result, it's now far easier to get most people to advocate politically on behalf of a *for-profit* company than it is to get them to go vote in their own self-interest. But it stands to reason that if they're willing to advocate for a company, they'd bother to vote too—provided it's just as easy.

And if Uber and FanDuel were useful indicators, what about having gone through the torturous process of trying to figure out how to run Mike Bloomberg for president? Mike could never run for president as a Republican or a Democrat because his views are out of sync with primary voters in each party. However, Mike's views actually align far closer to the average American voter's than most candidates who are just trying to seem as extreme as possible to appeal to primary voters. But because Mike couldn't compete as a member of either party, winning the electoral college was essentially impossible. That meant we ended up with Donald Trump in the White House—a pretty steep cost to maintain the status quo.

And finally, our work in our own backyard has made the need abundantly clear. More than 8.5 million people live in New York City. In the 2013 Democratic primary for mayor, just 691,000 people voted. The winner—Bill de Blasio—captured 282,000 votes, and as the Democrat, the general election was a fait accompli. As a result, de Blasio was effectively elected with 282,000 votes in a city of 8.5 million people. He knows that, and his governance has been solely designed to appeal to those 282,000 people, even at the expense of the other 8.2 million. The same thing happened again in 2017, with de Blasio winning 320,000 votes in the Democratic primary and effectively again capturing the mayoralty as a result. This is not an anomaly, nor is it exclusive to members of one party or one jurisdiction. It's exactly how candidates are elected—and then govern—across the country at every level of government—municipal, county, state, federal—in every branch of government (executive, legislative, and, in many places, judicial).

The combination of these three events made it clear to me something has to be done if we want a government that can actually govern for the mainstream in an efficient way. Exponentially expanding participation in elections is the only way to do it. (If we change the inputs, we change the outputs.)

And while the idea is radical, it also isn't that different from everyday life. We all perform complicated transactions on our phones every single day—we move money around, buy goods and services, and express our views and ideas. For most of us, our phone is more than a utility—it's indispensable. And yet when it comes to the act most fundamental to maintaining our democracy, we toss aside the object we rely upon most and revert instead to an outdated approach that is difficult from start to finish—from identifying your polling place, to finding time to go there, waiting in line, dealing with confused/hostile people working at the polling place, finally voting, and then driving or walking back to wherever you started. If all voting requires is opening up an app on your phone, a lot more people will do it.*

It probably goes without saying that those who like things the way they are—in other words, every current politician, interest group, union, major donors, and anyone else who has no interest in making it easier for people to challenge their power—will raise a host of objections to mobile voting. People who spent a lifetime figuring out how to capture and stay in office don't want to suddenly make it easier for anyone to challenge them and possibly win. They can't admit that

---

* In fact, it's fair to argue that when there's one vehicle for voting that's widespread and easily accessible (the phones already in your pocket) and another that's far more difficult to use (making people go someplace), you're effectively restricting the people's right to vote by only permitting the far more difficult option.

they're afraid of competition so they'll come up with the same flimsy excuses we see from entrenched interests afraid of competition from startups. They'll say it's too dangerous. (Of course, they also couldn't define blockchain if their next election depended on it.) They'll say not everyone has access to smartphones. (It'd be far cheaper to just buy them for everyone than to run a government this inefficient and this ineffective because no one bothers to vote.) They'll enlist all of their institutional donors and supporters (trade groups, unions, local party organizations) to whine and moan about how risky it'd be to change the status quo.

Beating those excuses back is going to take a long time (this is probably a ten- to twenty-year project) and it's going to mean having rock-solid answers to their concerns about hacking, especially as concerns about foreign interference in U.S. elections via Facebook, Google, and Twitter only grow. It's going to mean changing laws in each state to allow for mobile voting, developing a model set of election rules, policies, and procedures that can be adapted for each jurisdiction, finding a few jurisdictions willing to conduct a pilot program to give the idea a try, and convincing major social platforms, as well as the device developers themselves, to help out by constantly reminding their users to vote. It probably will require federal legislation too.

In other words, I knew what needed to be done. But it was a lot to take on, and a plan on paper alone wasn't going to accomplish much. I couldn't run Tusk Ventures and try to make mobile voting happen in my spare time. So I hired someone who could.

When Sheila Nix came to work for us in the governor's office in Illinois in 2004, after I took a look at her résumé and spent some time with her, I felt like I should be reporting to her and not the other way around. Sheila had served as the chief of staff to two U.S. senators— Bob Kerrey and Bill Nelson. She served as the executive director of Bono's One Foundation. She was Jill Biden's chief of staff during the second Obama term. She was our policy director in Illinois and then succeeded me as deputy governor. And like Bob Greenlee and me, she was an alum of the University of Chicago Law School. We kept in touch, and as the Obama administration was wrapping up, we started talking about what she should do next. She wanted to work on something big and meaningful, have autonomy to run it, work with people she knew and liked, and stay involved in politics without having to deal with all of the nonsense that came with working directly for a politician. I had a pretty good idea of a role that might fit her needs.

Sheila joined us as president of Tusk Montgomery Philanthropies in 2017, handling both our work on hunger (we fund and run campaigns around the country to pass legislation expanding funding for programs like school breakfast; so far we've had success in Pennsylvania, North Carolina, Illinois, Washington State, New Jersey, Tennessee, and New York)* and getting mobile voting off the ground.

We felt pretty qualified to get things going: We work in tech, we work in politics, we weren't worried about pissing off either political party, and our experiences in mobilizing people for our startups meant we knew the terrain. Between my weekly columns, my podcast, and all of the speeches I give at events and conferences, we had a platform to promote the concept. And while someone like Mike Bloomberg or Reid Hoffman will probably have to pick up the mantle once we need to start funding campaigns in every state to make mobile voting a reality, I could at least dedicate the financial resources to finding the right platforms, convincing election officials to give it a try, and proving it could work somewhere.

---

* I should give credit where it's due, again to Mike Bloomberg and his team at Bloomberg Philanthropies: Patti Harris, Howard Wolfson, and Allison Jaffin. Tusk Montgomery Philanthropies is effectively a derivative spinoff of what they're doing: using our money and political skill to fight for broad social change around causes we care about. The scope is exponentially bigger at the mothership but their ideas seem to work at all levels.

It's the early days. We've met some promising startups using block-chain to make mobile voting secure and possible. We've talked to election officials in the states of Washington, Montana, West Virginia, Colorado, Illinois, and Vermont, who are at least willing to consider the concept. We've talked to the Department of Defense about trying out a pilot for deployed members of the military. We've created a working group of advocates, startups, and blockchain experts. And we put our first points on the board by working with Mac Warner, West Virginia's secretary of state, to conduct a mobile voting pilot for deployed military for their May 2018 primary. While most elected officials won't want to embrace change and make it easier for others to unseat them, there are always a few outliers like Mac and his team and we need to work with every single one of them.

There's no doubt that restoring our true democracy—and actually confronting our nation's deepest problems—resides with changing the way people vote. Whether or not we have the ability to change the way the people see mobile voting is an open question. If we're as good at running campaigns as we say, then over time, we ought to be able to pull this off. But it's a lot heavier lift than legalizing fantasy sports or online insurance or weed delivery or ridesharing.

Technology and history should both be on our side. But everyone invested in the status quo clearly will do everything they can to stop us. And that may make this the biggest disruption fight of all.

A Quick Guide to Startup Politics

If You're a Startup Facing:

1. Trying to decide whether to ask for permission or beg for forgiveness

   Ask yourself:

   - What's the jurisdiction? Is it a place you should be able to work with or are they intractable/corrupt and a fight is required?
     - There's a reason why Illinois, New Jersey, Rhode Island, and Louisiana have the reputations they do.

   - Can you count on grassroots support from your customers?

   - How is your narrative compared to whomever you're disrupting? Can the press influence the regulators and politicians? Will they care enough to bother?
     - This gets back to your relative goodness versus theirs and whether your issue is interesting enough for reporters to care.

- What are the existing laws on the books? If you beg for forgiveness, is it at least arguable that the law was fine in the first
  place?

  ◦ This is a really important point—you don't have to concede that
    the law as written outlaws what you want to do. Just because it's
    silent (if the regulator could have envisioned whatever you ended
    up doing, she'd be an entrepreneur and not a bureaucrat) doesn't
    mean the tie goes to the runner and the entrenched interest gets
    to ban you from competing. It's possible the law as written pro-
    hibits what you want, but that's very different from not having
    explicit permission.

- From whom are you begging forgiveness? A regulator? A judge? A
  jury? Could you end up in jail?

  ◦ There are risks worth taking and risks not worth taking. As some-
    one who has testified in three trials and two grand juries, I can tell
    you that even being a witness is awful.

- How politically powerful and sophisticated are your opponents?
  How likable are they? How much money do they hand out? How are
  they viewed by the public?

  ◦ We've covered this above too, but the upshot is you need to under-
    stand the political strengths and reach of whomever you're dis-
    rupting.

- How important is this? Do you really want to take on this fight? How
  committed are you? Do you run the risk of going halfway, angering
  the people who regulate you without doing enough to actually force
  their hand?

  ◦ If you do it, do it right.

2. Inaction from regulators who don't know how to interpret what you do under current law (or simply refuse to do so)

Ask yourself:

- Why are they stalled? Is it out of genuine confusion, bureaucratic intransigence, or regulatory capture?

  - Sometimes they're being instructed by the politician who appointed them to keep you at bay. Sometimes they just hate change. Sometimes they're subject to regulatory capture. (Think Stockholm syndrome for regulators where they do the bidding of the people they're supposed to regulate.) And sometimes they're just genuinely confused. It's hard to know how to proceed and how to fight if you don't understand what's driving them.

- Did they decide to put the brakes on or were they instructed to do so by the elected official they report to? If the latter, is there a way to make this about pay-to-play?

  - Look at the campaign donations from the interest you're disrupting to the politician who appointed the regulator screwing with you.

- Does your model open up a regulatory/legislative can of worms? (In other words, do they have a valid reason for delay/concern?)

  - While there's almost always a political reason for why you're facing trouble, there may also be a legitimate policy reason. You need to understand what it is and develop a reasonable, workable solution.

- What will it take to move them? Do you need a big public fight? Just some nudging internally? Do you need to embarrass them? And do you have the weapons to credibly do so?

    ◦ In other words, you need a campaign and a campaign strategy. This may be something you can solve with a good lobbyist. Or you may need all guns blazing—earned media, social media, paid media, opposition research, and grassroots. You can't win if you don't even know what weapons you need to bring to the fight.

- If you succeed in moving them, how does that impact you in other jurisdictions? Can you use it as a precedent and validation?

    ◦ Some places are more important than others. Fights in major media markets get noticed elsewhere. Policy agreements or political fights with high-profile politicians get noticed elsewhere. If you're looking to pick your battles or send a message, this all needs to be taken into account.

3. A decision whether to try to mobilize your customers to advocate for you politically

Ask yourself:

- How much do your customers care about what you offer them?

    ◦ Are your customers truly passionate about your product/service? Can they live without it? Saying no doesn't mean you don't have a great business. It's just that some things inspire political action more than others. Misunderstanding that can lead to a lot of wasted time and money. What's the incumbent like? How strong is the juxtaposition between what you offer and what they offer?

    ◦ If the competition offers a really crappy product and your alternative is dramatically better (think taxi compared to Uber), the risk of having to go back to the old way is often enough to motivate people to act. If the distinction is less severe, grassroots may not work.

- Do you have enough customers to move the needle if mobilized? (Assume you're only going to get 5 to 10 percent of them involved no matter how good the political dynamic.)

  ○ It's possible that you meet all the criteria to mobilize your customers but it won't matter because you just don't have that many of them yet. It's hard to assume more than 5 percent or so of the people you ask to advocate will actually do so. So if you only have three hundred customers in a market, fifteen tweets may not do much to help.

- Do the electeds involved care about your customers? Are they prime voters? Are they at all politically active/aware?

  ○ Not all of your customers are viewed equally in the eyes of your regulator. The only ones who matter are those who vote—or at least could vote if they were sufficiently outraged. While whomever you're advocating to probably won't check the voter records of each person who tweets at them, the more local your advocacy, the better.

- Can you credibly threaten to turn your customer base into a political force? Can you register them to vote? Keep them informed and motivated? Present a credible electoral threat? Conduct a real get-out-the-vote operation?

  ○ It's great to know how to try to scare a politician. It's not likely to work if they don't think you know how to deliver on the threat. You at least need to have the resources lined up so your claims are credible.

4. How to layer in a political analysis into your market-expansion strategy

Ask yourself:

- What are the laws on the books around your issue?

  ○ Some jurisdictions may already permit what you want, some may have laws that are silent, some may prohibit it. You should know this before deciding what markets to enter.

- How powerful is whomever you're disrupting in that market?

  ○ If you're trying to decide between multiple cities, your opponent is not uniformly powerful or powerless in each. It changes by jurisdiction. You need to know how they stack up in each place.

- How much does the elected official in charge want to seem pro-innovation?

  ○ This is a combination of looking at their rhetoric (speeches, op-eds, campaign promises), actions (what they've actually done while in office around tech), and political ambitions. (How much does having genuine tech accomplishments help propel them to the next job?)

- If you succeed in that market, do other cities/states or mayors/governors follow their lead?

  ○ While all mayors and governors see themselves as great leaders, some resonate much more with their colleagues than others. Picking jurisdictions that others want to emulate always helps.

- What media market is it in? How much will a fight in that market help/hurt your profile and narrative?

- ° If you're going to invest time and money into a fight, you should use it to send a message everywhere else. That means, if possible, conducting the fight in a place where people pay attention (New York, Los Angeles, San Francisco, Washington D.C., or Chicago).

- Are there any relevant supporters of yours in that market (investors especially)?

  - ° You may not have any preexisting resources that are useful in a regulatory fight but you should at least survey what you have (investors, personal relationships) and make sure you note anything that could help.

5. An attack from an entrenched interest you're disrupting

Ask yourself:

- How sympathetic are they to the public, the media, regulators, and customers? What's their narrative about why limiting competition from you makes sense?

  - ° Some entrenched interests are already seen as sleazy (taxi medallion owners, casinos) and it's easy to counter their political influence. Others (affordable housing advocates) are seen as sympathetic and it's tougher.

  - ° If the public knows and hates the product/service provided by whomever you're disrupting, it's a much easier fight. (If the product/service is beloved, you presumably wouldn't be trying to disrupt it anyway.) Checking their Net Promoter Score is one quick way to tell.

- How politically influential are they? Based on what? Campaign do-nations or something more? Does the elected official(s) in charge of your issue fear them?

  ○ Look at how much money they've donated and to whom. Are they major donors? Over what period of time? (This sounds compli-cated but anyone with access to the Internet can find most of the information pretty easily—there are a slew of websites that reveal campaign donations both by specific people and to specific candi-dates.)

  ○ If your enemy has real political power—can turn out votes in an election, their endorsement matters, can influence public opinion—it's much tougher than if they just have deep pockets and expect their largess to protect them from you.

- How ethical are they? Can you turn their strength (campaign contri-butions) into a weakness (corruption)?

  ○ While politicians are desperate for campaign cash, there are very few donors important enough to risk a story alleging corruption over. More than $100,000 in donations may sound like a lot, but a three-day story about pay-to-play politics does more political harm than the donation does good.

- How important is their well-being to the agenda and policy goals of the elected official(s) you need?

  ○ If you're Airbnb, for example, and the politician trying to rein you in has made affordable housing a top issue, that's a problem. But if you're a bike-share startup and that's not something the mayor has ever even talked about, it should be a little easier.

- Who else can they bring to the fight? Do they have powerful allies or can they be isolated?

○ Unsympathetic but smart opponents will line up others to do their bidding. If they can rally clergy, unions, policy advocates, and the like to their side, it gives the politician they control more cover to screw you over. If they're isolated, it's harder.

6. A decision whether to take on a political fight in any given jurisdiction

Ask yourself:

• What tools do you have at your disposal?

○ Can you solve the problem by hiring a good lobbyist? If so, do you know how to manage a lobbyist?

Keep in mind, the real client for most lobbyists is not you—it's the elected official you're asking them to lobby. They usually have a lot more clients who want something from an elected official than political capital with that elected official. So the name of the game is to mete out progress, keep the retainer coming, juggle each client's priorities, and not expend too much capital on behalf of any one of them. The antidote is to manage them very aggressively, require constant progress, and force them to spend their capital on you.

○ Do you have the moral high ground? Can you frame your opponent and the politician doing their bidding as corrupt?

We've covered this already above, but the trick here is to turn their strength into a weakness—it's much harder for them to use their political contributions as leverage against you if the politician they donated to is being called out publicly for corruption.

○ How interested is the press in your issue? Can you generate enough coverage to make a difference?

Just because you find something interesting or important doesn't mean the media will. Reporters tend to like covering process and politics. (Policy is tough to cover these days.) Scandals, corruption, hypocrisy, and new gadgets usually work too.

○ How much money can you dedicate to this fight? Enough to run a real campaign? Buy TV ads? Radio? Direct mail? Digital?

The first question is how important the fight is in the first place. Far too many startups go in half-cocked, spend some money, get no results, lose their fight, and end up worse off than when they started. Know what success looks like, what it will likely take and cost, then decide. (And once you do, do it right.)

○ Can you successfully mobilize your customers to advocate for you?

○ Do you have any other assets that are politically valuable? Can you offer or threaten jobs? Tax revenue?

You may have more weapons than you realize. Threaten to move your headquarters. Threaten to close your local office. Talk about how other cities/states are more tech-friendly and deserve your jobs more. Show what the city/state stands to lose long-term if you leave.

○ Can you build a coalition? Is this a true consumer-rights issue? Will other advocates come to your defense?

Americans don't like being told where they can and can't shop, what they can and can't do with their cars, their homes, their stuff. Property rights are underappreciated as a narrative and advocacy tool.

○ Are there other political dynamics at play that can be useful? Did the same politician just crack down on a different startup and doesn't want to be branded as antitech? Can you side with them on another fight to back them off of your issue?

Sometimes timing really is everything. Let's say another startup just bit the dust in the same jurisdiction because the politician in charge was doing the bidding of a donor or entrenched interest. That could be your opportunity—most politicians don't want to be branded as antitech and anti-innovation, so if giving you a win helps them achieve that, you may be in luck. There's the old story of a bear chasing two guys in the woods. As they're fleeing, one guy says to the other, "You think we can outrun the bear?" The other guy responds, "I don't have to outrun the bear. I just have to outrun you." The more you understand the whole landscape, the better your odds of spotting who else is facing trouble and offering your solution as a way for the politician in question to minimize the political harm.

7. An attack from a politician who takes money from whomever you're disrupting

Ask yourself:

- Where is the attack coming from? Is it motivated by policy goals or just donor demands?

  ◦ Most politicians do have issues they care about—even if they're not willing to risk their political career over it. If this is a genuine issue of interest for the elected official regulating you, it's a tougher fight because they'll expend more capital to win. If they're just taking care of a donor, going through the motions may be enough.

- How does the attack fit with the elected's overall agenda? Can you turn their own narrative against them?

  ◦ The press loves unmasking hypocrisy. If the attack against you contradicts what the elected has said publicly in the past (look at their speeches, interviews, press releases, Twitter feeds, campaign promises, debate transcripts, etc.), that can be a very powerful lever.

- How strong is your narrative? How sympathetic is your position to the public (and the media)? What type of coalition of supporters can you build?

  ◦ If you can point to a way the public is currently being mistreated (overcharged, underserved) and show that your product/service helps solve the problem, that's a good narrative. It's even better if you can align yourself with groups already upset about the problem (consumer advocates, issue advocates, unions, or clergy).

- Can you devote real resources to the fight? How much money? Can you pay for ads? Events? PR? Do you have the right internal resources and expertise?

  ◦ This stuff can be expensive. You need to know up front how important winning is to you, how much it truly matters, and how much a real campaign will cost. It may be that survival requires victory and you'll do whatever it takes. But maybe not.

  ◦ And this is the time to know what you don't know. Just because you're really smart doesn't mean you understand politics. At all. And just because your general counsel went to law school, reads *Politico*, watches MSNBC, and volunteered for Obama in 2008 doesn't mean she does either. You wouldn't hire a marketing expert to build your software. Take this just as seriously.

- Can you mobilize your customers to weigh in on your behalf? Do they care enough to do so? Do you have the tools and narrative to educate, motivate, and mobilize them?

  ○ First things first, be honest. Are your customers truly passionate about your product/service? Can they live without it? Saying no doesn't mean you don't have a great business. It's just that some things inspire political action more than others. Misunderstanding that can lead to a lot of wasted time and money.

  ○ Assuming they do care, you need the tools to actually mobilize them. If at all possible, do it from the app. That's when you have their attention. It's when they're most likely to help you. And make it easy—advocating on your behalf (email, Twitter, Instagram) shouldn't take more than one or two clicks.

8. A decision to shape regulations for an entirely new sector that currently lacks them

Ask yourself:

- What would the right regulations look like? How do you know? Is the answer "none"? If so, can you truly support and sell that publicly?

  ○ Either you're going to figure out the rules and do the politics right to enact them or someone is going to do it for you. Be wary of participating in endless government and trade association working groups (although most general counsels love them). Little gets done.

- Who should regulate you? At what level of government? Which agencies?

  ◦ This is really important—the laws that create the regulatory structure will also set out who regulates you. This can be the difference between war and peace, between someone who understands what you're trying to do and someone who hates change.

- What are the best test cases to pursue (cities, counties, states)? Who is the friendliest audience? Where will you face the least initial opposition?

  ◦ Not all jurisdictions are the same. But the first few to act are likely to see their work replicated widely. So take the time to do the research, analyze the options, understand the underlying politics, and then decide.

- Who has the most efficient rule-making process? Can you create regulations without passing legislation?

  ◦ These are more technical questions but the difference between a regulation and legislation could be at least twelve months.

- What kind of campaign do you need to succeed? What does the inside game look like? How about the outside game? Do you have the resources and tools to execute them?

Cast of Characters

Where Are They Now (as of March 2018)– and What Can We Learn from Them?

MIKE BLOOMBERG

CEO of Bloomberg L.P. Chairman of Bloomberg Philanthropies. National/global leader on climate change, gun safety, immigration reform, education reform, and public health. Ranked #6 on the Forbes list of the richest people in the United States.

Key takeaway: He does what he thinks is right without worrying what other people think. He understood that the best way to govern was as if every term was your last and if you make a decision based on its merits, the public will usually respect it. He's also incredibly generous and decent, and his management style reflects that completely. (I've copied it in every way possible.) He is the most impressive person I have ever worked for or with.

CHUCK SCHUMER

Minority leader of the U.S. Senate. Seen as the leader of the Democratic fight against Donald Trump. Likely Senate majority leader one day. (The 2018 map is tough, but you never know.)

Key takeaway: His relentlessness is admirable, even if exhausting. His pace, ability to spot opportunities and take advantage of them, creativity, and work ethic are all worth emulating. Obviously, his life would be easier (although less well known) if he didn't have such a deep need for constant attention.

TRAVIS KALANICK

Stepped down as CEO of Uber in June 2017. Remains among the company's largest shareholders.

Key takeaway: His vision, relentlessness, courage, creativity, and mettle are all legendary. His biggest failing, in my view, was not adapting his style as Uber shifted from a scrappy startup to a $68 billion company.

ROD BLAGOJEVICH

In the middle of a fourteen-year prison sentence for corruption. He will likely be released from jail in 2024 (depending on good behavior) at the age of sixty-three. However, Trump has been musing about commuting Rod's sentence (as of this writing) so by the time you're reading this, he could be out.

Key takeaway: Obviously, there are a lot more lessons here on what not to do than what to do. (You should not forget to come into the office for three months at a time; you should not constantly look to see how every situation can provide you with personal financial gain.) But to his credit, Rod was really tough, had world-class political skills, and allowed us to create and launch a lot of good policies. (Even the worst public officials usually have some areas where they've done some good.)

ED RENDELL

After serving as mayor of Philadelphia, he went on to serve as governor of Pennsylvania and as chair of the Democratic National Committee. Now writes books, practices law, and is a regular on a TV show about the Philadelphia Eagles.

Key takeaway: Like Chuck Schumer and Travis Kalanick, Rendell was relentless, and his constant advocacy for Philadelphia really helped transform the city. (Buzz Bissinger's *A Prayer for the City* about Rendell's quest in Philly is worth reading.) His willingness to just speak his mind was also admirable (especially for a politician). I didn't work for him closely enough to know firsthand what not to emulate.

HENRY STERN

Retired from city government in 2000. Founded New York Civic, a good-government organization. Has been largely retired the past few years. Harper and I were happy to endow the Henry J. Stern Scholarship at his alma mater, City College—a full scholarship awarded each year to a student pursuing a career in city government.

Key takeaway: His absolute love for New York City's Parks, playgrounds, trees, wildlife, zoos, lakes, recreation centers, and everything else in the Emerald Empire was astounding. So was his work ethic, intelligence, and creativity. On the other hand, his personal views on race, gender, and ethnicity were both backward and offensive to many, and he lacked the discipline and self-awareness to either evolve his thinking or just keep his opinions to himself.

ANTHONY WEINER

Sentenced in 2017 to serve twenty-one months in federal prison for illegal sexual contact with a minor. Resigned from Congress in 2010 after his Twitter scandal unfolded. Ran for mayor of New York City in 2013 and finished in fourth place after a new scandal emerged. Is blamed by Hillary Clinton for her presidential campaign loss in 2016, as investigations into his sexual allegations uncovered emails relating to the investigation around her using a private email server.

Key takeaway: It's hard to ascribe many positive traits to Anthony, but he was creative, energetic, and politically talented.

RAHM EMANUEL

Left the House of Representatives in 2008 to serve as chief of staff to President Obama. Was elected mayor of Chicago in 2011 and reelected in 2015. Despite suffering low approval ratings and several major controversies, he has endured, accomplished a lot, and is favored to win a third term in 2019.

Key takeaway: Rahm combines incredible intelligence, street smarts, savvy, creativity, and endless drive. His view of everything as political is typical for his profession, but still limits his appeal and probably his long-term prospects.

BILL DE BLASIO

Reelected to a second term in November 2017. Narrowly avoided indictment for corruption. Will likely run for something else (the White House if possible) as soon as his term ends.

Key takeaway: He managed both to stay out of jail and to get reelected as mayor. His focus on pre-K and affordable housing are both admirable. Everything else about him is sad for the people of New York City. (We get what we deserve and by not bothering to vote, we probably deserve someone like de Blasio.)

ANDREW CUOMO

Still the governor of New York. May run for president in 2020. Lives to play the political chessboard, which makes him a perfect case study for how startups should approach their regulatory challenges.

Key takeaway: Chuck, Rahm, Rendell, Travis, and Andrew all have the same combination of drive, intensity, focus, ambition, intelligence, and savvy (although in differing degrees) that makes them very successful. I wouldn't want to have a beer with Andrew, but he's been a pretty good governor.

FANDUEL

Operates in forty states. Its proposed merger with DraftKings was rejected by the Federal Trade Commission in 2017. Its future will be heavily linked to the likelihood of sports betting being legalized in states across the nation.

Key takeaway: If you're going to take away market share from the casinos, be prepared for a really big fight.

HANDY

Operates in thirty-four markets in the United States, Canada, and the UK. Valued at $300 million and is pursuing worker-classification reform across the nation to be able to provide benefits to its professionals and have legal clarity from regulators. Oisin Hanrahan remains Handy's CEO.

Key takeaway: A CEO with vision and tenacity can not only build a business but also accomplish real policy change. Oisin has done that. It's not easy.

LEMONADE

Continues to grow rapidly. Recently raised their Series C funding round, with SoftBank as the lead investor at a valuation of $580 million. Daniel Schreiber remains CEO.

Key takeaway: If you give people a product that's easier, faster, cheaper, more attractive, and more appealing than the alternative, they're going to use it. Doing it in insurance is especially brilliant given the size of the industry and the calcification of its status quo. Daniel and Shai Wininger, his cofounder, also fully appreciated the importance of getting the politics right, and that's one of many reasons why Lemonade has been so successful.

UBER

Stabilized its leadership crisis in late 2017, sold 14 percent of its shares to SoftBank, continues to operate globally, appointed Dara Khosrowshahi to replace Travis as CEO, and has announced a tentative plan to conduct an initial public offering in 2019.

Key takeaway: When something is clearly not working as well as it should (taxi), the opportunity is there to introduce something better. But doing so doesn't just mean having a superior product: It means having the vision, audacity, tenacity, drive, and courage to see it through. Also, you're never as good as they say you are on your best day and you're rarely as bad as they make you out to be on your worst day.

EAZE

Continues to expand within California, continues to seek permission from each city to conduct delivery. Long-term success depends on staying afloat until the federal rules on cannabis change.

Key takeaway: I believe cannabis should be legal, and Eaze makes that case very elegantly through its service. Whether or not any one specific cannabis tech startup succeeds, ultimately the norms will change everywhere and the sector will succeed as a whole—but not until Trump leaves the White House.

MYTABLE

Nowhere. They went broke.

Key takeaway: If you're going to radically disrupt a long-accepted model of regulation, make sure you have enough money to survive the time it takes to change everyone's minds.

TESLA

Introducing new products and ideas. Elon's other big ideas, like SpaceX, The Boring Company, and Hyperloop, are also making real progress. Still can't sell direct to consumers in some states.

Key takeaway: Much of Tesla's (and Elon's) success comes from its brand. But sometimes, at least in politics, winning a tough fight means making things ugly, and that may conflict with the protect-the-brand-at-all-costs mentality. Sometimes you have to choose.

CARE/OF

Still growing and selling vitamins to millennials and other consumers.

Key takeaway: Startups that understand their customers and how to appeal to them in new ways are going to sell a lot more product.

Acknowledgments

This list is probably way too long, but who knows if I'll get to write another book. First and foremost, I want to thank my wife, Harper Montgomery, for being there with me throughout every step of this journey (not just the book but everything that happened in it) and supporting me emotionally and intellectually at every turn. I also want to thank Abigail and Lyle, my wonderful children, who just make me really, really happy every single day.

A lot of people helped to make this book possible, starting with my editor, Niki Papadopoulos; my agent, Kirsten Neuhaus; everyone at Portfolio Books, especially Adrian Zackheim, and everyone at Foundry Literary Media; our great illustrator, Shyama Golden; and my friend and talented photographer Charlie Gross, who did the impossible (managed to make me look not that awful in the author photo). A number of people from my team helped with the research, editing, publicity, graphics, legal review, and moral support for this book, including Meaghan Collins, Virginie Raphael, Christina Cioffe, Jennifer Hanley, Michaela Balderson, Jackie Zupsic, Patrick Muncie, Lance Trover, Bob Greenlee, Chris Coffey, Matt Yale, Seth Webb, Menashe Shapiro, Haley Rubinson, Marla Kanemitsu, Sheila Nix, and, of course, my sister, friend, closest adviser, and the person I fear the most, Marla Tusk. Thank you also to my friends at Management 360, Guymon Casady and Ben Forkner. There were also a number of people who read drafts that really weren't ready for primetime and gave me a lot of edits along the way: Howard Wolfson, Rich Zabel, Patrick Brennan, Jane Isay, Chris Peters, and Tom Heller.

As the book describes, I got a lot of lucky breaks and a lot of help from a lot of people over the years. Mike Bloomberg, Patti Harris, Kevin Sheekey, and Ed Skyler taught me what government and service can be and should be. Henry Stern, Ron Stack, Brian O'Dwyer, Eric Blinderman, Shelley Capito Macleod, Christian Goode, John Wyma, and so many others helped me along the way. I'm grateful to them. Special thanks to my parents, Gabe and Nadine Tusk; my brother-in-law, Josh Gottheimer (who meets the Bloomberg definition of service); my mother-in-law, Peggy Manley; and my sister-in-law, Cile Montgomery, for their encouragement (and in spirit, the late, great Larry Paul Manley).

And without any particular reason or order, some other people I want to thank for their friendship and help along the way: Ellie Gottheimer, Ben Gottheimer, Gray Maloney, Phillips Nazro, Neal Friske, Rob Galligan, Susan Scarimbolo, Elliot Regenstein, Emily Paster, Stuart Ruderfer, David Cohn, Cas Holloway, Bob Lawson, Melissa Barkan, Paul LeBlanc, Aleca Le Blanc, Ross Wallin, Andrea Begel, Erick Berreondo, Garrett Wotkyns, Dimitri Karcazes, Mark Moller, Jon Ackerman, Ben Lawsky, Shea Fink, Allison Jaffin, Josh Isay, Bill Knapp, Dan Heimowitz, Peter Madonia, John Crotty, Maura Keaney, Micah Lasher, Josh Mohrer, Jordan Nof, Matt King, Amber Morgan, Tom Tobin, Kim Holly, Sally Susman, Ven Medabalmi, Brandie Olseth, Loren Schlachet, Eric Monsowitz, Itay Feldman, Jeff Neuman, Patricia Machado, Joel Klein, Parke Spencer, Cathie Levine, Katy Gaul, Byron Stiggie, Jamie Rubin, Michael Eisenberg, Eden Shochat, Nina Sovich, Florent Latour, Andy Ross, Shari Roth, Rohan Hales, Larry Zelnick, Marc and Rhonda Marinoff, Luis Saenz, Rob Kelter, Eric Harmon, Bo Lauder, Rabbi Larry Sebert, Doug Perry and everyone at Common Table, Boyd Johnson, Doug Maynard, Brent Montgomery, Hugo Lindgren, Sarah Bernard, John Brennan, Jay Carson, Michelle Rhee, Miriam Corea, Shorne Smith, Jef Pollock, Deb Brown, Dave Allee, Elaine Cohen, Eileen and Dennis Sevano,

Perri and Brenna Sevano, Eric Tash and Greg Barlow, Patrick Jenkins, Mike Avella, Marissa Shorenstein, Oliver Schweitzer, Amanda Brokaw, Stu Loeser, Marc LaVorgna, Ian Shapiro, Abby Ottenhoff, Brian Daly, the late, great Ed Koch, Bill Taubman and the whole Taubman family, Brian Miller, Christian Genetski, David Grandeau, Frank Bruni, Lou Susman, Megan Sheekey, Caitlin LaCroix, Marcus Reese, Max Long, Jenna Matecki, Geoff Hutchinson, Melissa Heuer, Julijana Englander, Barry Zyskind, Adam Karkowsky, Jeff Fenster, Maggie Haberman, Stefan Friedman, Jennifer Cunningham, Bernice and Elliot Selig, Jay Marlin, Noel Taylor, Brian Flanagan, Jack Lavin, Merin Curotto, Kelsey Smith, Jon Fine, Marissa Dwyer, Patrick Chun, Jed Cairo, Brian Driscoll, Maureen Weiss, Michael Granoff, Matt Cleary, Daniella Landau, Dave Isay, Daniel Schreiber, Shai Wininger, Fred Yang, John Filan, Michelle Adams, Tim Tompkins, John Feinblatt, Gavin Wasserman, Matt Levine, Eran Shir, Kim Molstre, Justin Kintz, Colin Tooze, Solomon Hailu, Neil Giacobbi, Oisin Hanrahan, Jon Sabol, Josh Wachs, Scott Schwaitzberg, Seth London, Jay Zaveri, Paul Martino, Jenny Sedlis, Glen Weiner, Ken Kurson, Mike Matulis, Mitchell Moss, Anish Melwani, Linda Gibbs, Scott Pearl, Nick Daraviras, Jill Brienza, Yoni Rechtman, Quinn Shean, Dan Goff, Elizabeth Austin, Mary Lou Peters, Cass Sunstein, Dick Badger, Arnie Kriss, Eric Whitaker, Justin Marinoff, Gara Marinoff, Ishmael Bahmia, Louanner Peters, Julie Curry, Campbell Brown, Dan Senor, Jon Werbell, Jerry Speyer, Kelly Glynn, Tali Stein, Jeanne Arens, Nina Habib, Frank Rafaelle, Josh Mendelsohn, Julie Samuels, Alan Moss, Alexis Lipsitz, Royce Flippin, Dennis Walcott, Doug Sosnik, Barry Maram, Walter Robb, Becky Carroll, Megan Glenn, Jonathan Fanton, Lisa Quigley, Larry Harrington, Peter Taylor, Seth Coren, Brent Thompson, Joe Cini, Tom Collichio, Joe Williams, Marc Sternberg, Paul Jones, Fernando Grillo, Eva Moskowitz, Sam DePhillipo, Jon Werbell, Jerry Russo, Matt Wing, Peter Kaufmann, Jordan Barowitz, Kenny Kweku, Brian Ballard, Bernard Whitman, Doug Schoen, Frank Barry, Elizabeth Austin, Josh Sapan, Komal Ahmad, Charlie Schueler, Heidi Glunz, Malcolm Pinckney, Dave

Dring, Maria Whalen, Dan Doctoroff, Tom Cross, Tim Sullivan, Carol Ronen, Joe Handley, Costa Dimas, Diane Coffey, Pat Brown, Stacey Pfaff, Jake Goldman, Edward Isaac-Dovere, Dara Freed, Gary Ginsburg, David Greenfield, Judy Miller, Ray Hernandez, Rachel Holt, Carlo Scissura, Mason Plumlee, Taharka Robinson, Adam Riff, Karen Keough, Nigel Railton, Matt Mahoney, Reverend James Meeks, Andy Shaw, Mark Botnick, Ryan Whalen, Penny Lee, Greg Rost, Marc Matsil, Jen Skyler, Amelia Skyler, Annalise Skyler, Andrew Penson, Jim Anderson, Katherine Oliver, Anthony Crowell, Mike Levoff, Barnett Zitron, David Spielfogel, Mike Best, Haeda Mihaltses, Jesse Ruiz, Pat Lynch, Mike Murray, Ed Rendell, Jim Maiella, Jack Hartman, Maggie Sans, Steve Restivo, Bill Thorne, Reverend Mitchell Taylor, Rachel Whetstone, Steve Hilton, Anne Marie Murphy, Jason Post, Rebecca Rausch, Andrew Salkin, Max Young, Randy Dunn, Jon Banner, John Mackey, Ken Meyer, Pat Quinn, David Goldin, Dan Donovan, Craig Ebert, Kara Swisher, Vasuki Shastry, Jimmy Siegel, Miriam Hess, Colin Au, Gretchen Rubin, Connie Lozios, Reshma Saujani, Tim Brosnan, Craig Johnson, the Block-chain Trust Accelerator, Share Our Strength, Benefits Data Trust, all the LPs for Tusk Venture Partners, Erik Berge, Lindsay Zappala, Matya Schachter, Laura Alves, John O'Connor, Jessica Santos, Scott Galloway, Antonio García Martínez, Steven Soderbergh, and apologies (and drinks on me) for anyone I should have listed here but didn't.

Index